Law and Liberty:

A Biblical Look at Legalism

John MacArthur
Steven J. Lawson
Joel Beeke
Richard D. Phillips
Phil Johnson
Jim Elliff
Kenneth Talbot
Bruce Bickel
Don Kistler

Don Kistler, General Editor

The Northampton Press
... *for instruction in righteousness*...

A Division of Don Kistler Ministries, Inc.
P.O. Box 781135, Orlando, FL 32878-1135
www.northamptonpress.org

*

*

This book has been made possible through the generosity of John and Elise Maynard.

*

ISBN 978-0-9847062-1-1

*

Library of Congress Cataloging-in-Publication Data

Law and liberty : a biblical look at legalism / John MacArthur, Steven J. Lawson, Joel Beeke, Richard D. Phillips, Phil Johnson, Jim Elliff, Kenneth Talbot, Bruce Bickel, Don Kistler ; Don Kistler, general editor. -- First [edition].
    pages cm
  ISBN 978-0-9847062-1-1 (alk. paper)
  1. Grace (Theology)--Biblical teaching. 2. Liberty--Religious aspects--Christianity--Biblical teaching. 3. Law and gospel--Biblical teaching. 4. Law (Theology)--Biblical teaching. I. Kistler, Don, editor of compilation. II. Lawson, Steven J. Truth vs. tradition.
  BS2545.G73L39 2013
  241'.2--dc23
                                              2012049436

Contents

Contents

Author Bios

(The authors are listed in the order in which they appear.)

Dr. Don Kistler founded Soli Deo Gloria Publications in 1988 and The Northampton Press in 2007. He has written two books and edited more than 400 books, most of those first-time reprints of Puritan writings.

Dr. Steven J. Lawson is senior pastor of Christ Fellowship Baptist Church in Mobile, Ala. He is the author of 16 books and has pastored for over 30 years. Dr. Lawson is noted for his expository preaching.

Richard D. Phillips is the pastor of Second Presbyterian Church, Greenville, South Carolina. He chairs the Philadelphia Conference on Reformed Theology, founded by the late James Boice. He is the author of 21 books.

Dr. Bruce Bickel is the president and founder of Transformational Leadership Group. He is the author of *Light and Heat: The Puritan View of the Pulpit*.

Dr. John MacArthur has been the pastor/teacher of Grace Community Church in Southern California for 40 years. He also serves as president of the Master's College and Seminary. He has authored over 400 books and study guides.

Dr. Joel Beeke is the founder and president of Puritan Reformed Theological Seminary in Grand Rapids, Michigan. He serves as professor of systematic theology and homiletics. He is also pastor of Heritage Netherlands Reformed Congregation in Grand Rapids. He has written, co-authored, or edited over 70 books.

Dr. Kenneth Talbot is president of Whitefield College and Theological Seminary and serves as professor of theology and apologetics. He is a minister in the Reformed Presbyterian Church General Assembly (RPCGA) and is pastor of Christ Presbyterian Church in Lakeland, Florida. Whitefield College and Theological Seminary has offered degree programs through distance education for the past 32 years. Whitefield operates whitefieldmedia.com offering radio programs, video productions, and published books on various theological and philosophical subjects.

Phil Johnson is the executive director of Grace to You. He has been closely associated with John MacArthur since 1981 and edits most of John's major books. But he may be best known for several popular websites he maintains, including The Spurgeon Archive and The Hall of Church History. Phil has a bachelor's degree in theology from Moody Bible Institute (class of 1975) and was an editor at Moody Press before coming to Grace Community Church where he is an elder and pastors the Grace-Life fellowship group.

Jim Elliff is founder and president of Christian Communicators Worldwide (CCW). Since 1985 Jim has addressed Christian ministries, seminaries, Bible schools, universities, churches, and pastors' meetings throughout most of the United States and in many foreign countries. He is the author of four books that have been published in the U.S. and overseas, *Led by the Spirit, Pursuing God-A Seeker's Guide, Going Under: Discussions on Baptism, and Wasted Faith,* and was a co-author of *Divorce and Remarriage: A Permanence View.* In addition to his writing and travel, Jim began Christ Fellowship of Kansas City, Missouri in 2003, a unique church is made up of numerous home congregations in the Kansas City metro area.

Introduction

What Legalism Is, What Legalism Does

The late theologian Dr. John H. Gerstner, when talking about antinomianism, used to paraphrase a hymn by Philip Bliss as follows: "Free from the law, O blessed condition, I can sin as I please and still have remission."

This book is not about antinomianism, however, but about its equally deadly counterpart, legalism. There is a great need for a book on this topic, I believe.

Ask people to define "legalism" and you will likely get as many different definitions as people asked. It's a pejorative term that is thrown around a great deal in Christian circles, most often by someone trying to defend a certain behavior or trying to deflect a criticism of their behavior. One person might approach another person to confront him or her about an activity they believe to be wrong or sinful, only to hear this response: "I'm not interested in your legalism!" And the behavior in question may be legitimately and rightly pointed out as wrong according to Scripture, yet the accusation of legalism is supposed to end the discussion. Even if the confronting person can cite an explicit command or clear principle from God's Word, the predictable response is all too familiar: "Well, that's just your interpretation." The spiritual climate today is reminiscent of that tragic statement in the Bible describing the time of Judges when "everyone did what was right in his own eyes."

One typical definition of "legalism" is "an obsessive concern with rules." It may also be defined as "a tendency to pay more attention to the letter of the law than the spirit of the law." Someone else might suggest that a legalist is someone who is more concerned with law than with grace. All of those are common conceptions, and there's a bit of truth in each of them. But the real gist of the matter is much deeper than any of those defi-

1

nitions suggest. Let me offer another: Legalism is behavior motivated by the false notion that sinners can earn favor with God,
either before or after salvation, through legal means—obedience,
ritual, self-denial, or whatever.

There is a memorable scene in the movie "Saving Private
Ryan." Tom Hanks plays a captain who has been sent to rescue
Private Ryan (Matt Damon) from the war since three of his
brothers have already died in fighting. In this particular scene,
Captain Miller (Hanks) has been shot and is dying. Private Ryan
has been pulled out of the fighting and is to go home. He sees
that the man who saved his life is dying and leans over to hear
his last words, and they are telling: "Earn this. Earn it."

In essence, that's what legalism says: "Earn this," whether it's
salvation or sanctification. Legalism says that the presence of
certain behaviors or the absence of other ones can make us more
favorable to God, more worthy in God's eyes, than we might
otherwise be.

And even among those who rightly understand that salvation is a gift of God's free grace, apart from any merit of human
works, it is far too often the case that people think they can earn
or merit God's increased favor by what they do or don't do as
redeemed people. This is a terrible insult to the finished work of
Christ, for it is saying that what Christ accomplished for me is
not enough to receive God's favor, but what I do myself will
make up the difference.

Think of it. Christ suffered an infinite punishment for sin on
the cross, not at the hands of Roman soldiers, but at the hands of
His Father. As Isaiah 53:10 says: "It pleased the LORD to bruise
Him" (NKJV). It was God the Father who crushed God the Son
on the cross, as He bore the sins of all who would ever believe in
Him. For three hours Christ paid the excruciating penalty, and
an infinite penalty at that, of others' sins. The full force of God's
wrath was poured out on Him—infinite punishment in a finite
period of time, which intensified it all the more. And it was not
for one sin, or for one person's sin, but for each and every sin of

each and every person for whom Christ died, until finally it was done and He could utter those immortal words, "It is finished."

No impenitent sinner in hell will ever hear those words, because his or her punishment will never be finished. And no justified person in heaven will ever hear that what Christ did is now insufficient, for God has declared that He is satisfied. And if God is satisfied, He, who is immutable, can never be dissatisfied with what His Son has accomplished for sinners.

In other words, if God is satisfied, He is infinitely satisfied. And that is the only ground of acceptance with God for both sinners and saints. As Paul says in Ephesians 1:6, we are "accepted in the Beloved." We are accepted by God in Christ and because of Christ. Nothing about us is the basis for God accepting us. If God accepts a person, that person is fully accepted by God. Our acceptance with God depends solely on our being "in Christ," to use the Pauline phrase. The question is never how good I have been, but how good Christ has been on my behalf. So the question that begs to be asked is: How could a person possibly think to improve on what Christ has done? How could any rational being entertain the idea that something a sinner does might add anything to what Christ has done, whether it be with regard to salvation or sanctification?

Often, the things that someone given to legalism feels good about are peripheral matters, things such as dancing, drinking, smoking, or movies. There was a popular evangelical mantra a few years ago that went like this: "We don't drink, and we don't chew, and we don't hang with them what do!" There are some who actually believe they have more favor with God because they do not imbibe alcohol, participate in dancing, use tobacco, or attend movies of any kind. That kind of thinking says this: "What Christ did to satisfy your demands, O Lord, was good, I'll grant you that. But I've gone even further. I don't drink!"

I grant that there are some activities that a person could claim Scriptural backing for avoiding, and we would never want to bind or loose another person's conscience with regard to such things. If a person thinks something is wrong for him to do, then he cannot go against his conscience (see James 4:17). It only becomes problematic when such a person seeks to bind the conscience of another person, when they insist that their personal preference becomes someone else's precept. "I don't go to movies because I believe it is wrong to do so, and therefore it is wrong for YOU to do so."

There are so many instances of legalism that we could never possibly state them all. One young man with whom I was associated told his girlfriend that she was sinning because she wore high heels, which accentuated her calves, which made her more appealing to men, which caused them to lust. For some, skirts more than one inch above the knee are improper for a Christian. For others, all dancing is to be avoided, even square dancing. Card games are wrong, even such seemingly innocent ones as Rook and Old Maid, for no other reason than that they are card games. More examples are unnecessary, but they are legion.

In Luke 17, Jesus addressed this notion of earning God's favor with His disciples. It came in the context of His teaching on forgiveness. After He had told them how much they were to forgive (70 X 7), and how often (as often as they were asked), their response was, "We're going to need more faith!"

And then He said, "After you have done everything I have commanded you, say, 'We are unprofitable servants. We have only done our duty.' " Think of the implications of that statement for all of us. If we actually were to do *everything* that Christ commanded us to do, from the moment of our birth until the moment of our death, with nothing less than the motive of God's glory and our neighbor's good; if we never spoke an unkind word to anyone; if we were never unjustifiably angry with another person; if we fulfilled all our responsibilities inside as well as outside the home; if we always gave our employer eight hours work for eight hours pay; if we were perfect our entire life—we wouldn't even have earned a "thank you" from God. We would only have done our duty. God may acknowledge such righteous conduct some day with a "Well done, thou good and faithful servant," but we wouldn't have *earned* a thing.

It must follow, then, that if our *perfect* works could not earn God's favor, certainly our *imperfect* works cannot do so. And as the Puritan Thomas Taylor once wrote: "If our righteousness is filthy in God's sight, what must our sin be?"

The idea that something we do could make God look on us with more favor than He did simply because of the merits of Christ and His finished work is something that neither "the Bible nor evident reason," to use Luther's words, will support. No, the infinite merit of Jesus Christ is the basis for God's infinite favor with the believer. If that is not true, then Christ did not achieve the full satisfaction of God with His sufferings on the cross. And if that is the case, then nothing we could do could possibly make up the difference.

John Calvin once said, "Where the Scripture is silent, we may not speak." It is equally true that where the Scripture speaks, we may not argue. Legalism argues with Scripture and adds to it. Even worse, legalism says to Christ, "You got it started, but I'll take it from here." May it never be.

The authors in this compilation address the issue of legalism from a variety of angles.

John MacArthur shows, first, that obedience to God is not an issue of legalism, but an issue of love. In his second chapter, he deals with the inevitable response of people who are confronted with biblical standards, "Judge not that ye be not judged." Here MacArthur shows what our Lord meant when He said that, and shows what biblical discernment really is, that there is a vast difference between being judgmental and holding people accountable to God's standards.

Phil Johnson, in his first chapter, deals with Christian liberty. In his second chapter, he takes a critical look at two kinds of legalism, then explores the relationship of Christian love and Christian liberty.

Joel Beeke shows that enthusiasm for God's law is not necessarily legalism. One can be zealous without being legalistic. As David wrote: "Oh, how I love Thy law!"

Bruce Bickel explains that legalism is due to a weak understanding of what Christ accomplished on the cross.

Jim Elliff makes clear that legalism is an attack on unity within the Body of Christ, particularly local congregations.

Ken Talbot helps us to see that legalism is inconsistent with and incompatible with the doctrine of justification by faith alone. He points out that the doctrine of "free will" leads to this dangerous position.

Rick Phillips explores the relationship to loving God and obeying His law. Some today believe that love is all that matters, and that the law as a guideline to love is extinct. Then this author shows that Biblical sanctification is the antidote to and the opposite of legalism.

Steven J. Lawson shows that legalism is the result of holding to man-made traditions over the truth of God's Word. Second, he points out how dangerous and deadly a thing legalism is and why.

Truth Vs. Tradition
Dr. Steven J. Lawson

The Pharisees and some of the scribes gathered around Him when they had come from Jerusalem, and had seen that some of His disciples were eating their bread with impure hands, that is, unwashed. (For the Pharisees and all the Jews do not eat unless they carefully wash their hands, thus observing the traditions of the elders; and when they come from the market place, they do not eat unless they cleanse themselves; and there are many other things which they have received in order to observe, such as the washing of cups and pitchers and copper pots.) The Pharisees and the scribes asked Him, "Why do Your disciples not walk according to the tradition of the elders, but eat their bread with impure hands?" And He said to them, "Rightly did Isaiah prophesy of you hypocrites, as it is written: 'This people honors Me with their lips, But their heart is far away from Me. 'But in vain do they worship Me, Teaching as doctrines the precepts of men.' "Neglecting the commandment of God, you hold to the tradition of men." He was also saying to them, "You are experts at setting aside the commandment of God in order to keep your tradition. "For Moses said, ' Honor your father and your mother'; and, 'He who speaks evil of father or mother, is to be put to death'; but you say, 'If a man says to his father or his mother, whatever I have that would help you is Corban (that is to say, given to God),' you no longer permit him to do anything for his father or his mother; thus invalidating the word of God by your tradition which you have handed down; and you do many things such as that." (Mark 7:1–13)

Whenever the truth of the Word of God confronts those who are legalistic and bound by man-made rules as a strict code of conduct, a violent collision will inevitably result. Whenever

7

divine truth challenges human tradition, a fierce clash is un-
avoidable. Like a high and low pressure system colliding, a fierce
storm will surely erupt. Whenever the Scripture exposes empty
religion, there will always be a jarring conflict. The truth of God
is *that* provocative.

Such a conflict once shook Europe and ignited the Protestant
Reformation of the sixteenth century. It was the violent collision
caused by the return to biblical truth after centuries of empty
tradition. The noted church historian, Philip Schaff, describes
this crisis the following way:

> The objective principle of Protestantism maintains
> that the Bible, as the inspired record of revelation,
> is the only infallible rule of faith and practice; in
> opposition to the Roman Catholic coordination of
> Scripture and ecclesiastical *tradition*, as the joint
> rules of faith. The teaching of the living church is
> by no means rejected, but subordinated to the
> Word of God; while the opposite theory virtually
> subordinates the Bible to tradition. (*History of the
> Christian Church,* volume 7, 16-17)

This was the core issue of the Reformation in a nutshell,
namely the clash between truth and tradition. Schaff then notes:
"Every true progress in church history is conditioned by a new
and deeper study of the Scriptures." That is to say, whenever the
church moves forward in spiritual strength, such progress is always preceded by a decisive return to the authority of divine
truth. At such pivotal times, the traditions of the church are
made subject to the unvarnished truth of the Bible.

So the question must be asked, what is truth? And what is
tradition?

Truth is whatever God says something is. Simply put, truth
is reality. It is the way things really are. Truth is whatever is consistent with God Himself. It is that which is in perfect alignment
with His divine attributes and perfections. Truth is the self-

revelation of His own being. All truth is measured by the self-disclosure of God's own glory. In short, God Himself *is* truth.

This being so, God Himself is the sole Author of truth. God is the ultimate Source of truth. He alone is the exclusive Determiner, absolute Standard, and final Judge of all truth. The Bible says that God is "the God of truth" (Psalm 31:5), who is "abounding in truth" (Exodus 34:6). Jesus, likewise, is "the truth" (John 14:6). The Holy Spirit, moreover, is "the Spirit of truth" (John 14:17). The Bible is "truth" (John 17:17). Therefore, "All who worship God must do so in spirit and in truth" (John 4:24). No one can know God apart from the truth. Neither can anyone worship Him apart from the truth. Nor can anyone grow spiritually apart from the truth.

By contrast, tradition is any man-made religious rules and regulations contrary to the Word of God that must be kept for either salvation or sanctification. It is such tradition that fosters legalism. What is so deadly about legalistic tradition is that it supplants the truth and retards spiritual growth. Whenever anyone yields the high ground of truth and descends into the low places of tradition, the result is spiritual death and declension. No one can be saved or sanctified apart from the truth. Whenever tradition trumps truth, the mindless motions of dead religion result.

This conflict between truth and tradition is precisely what occurred in the days of Christ's first coming. The Pharisees and scribes had elevated their own religious rules above the inspired teaching of Scripture. In so doing, Jesus declared that the tradition of the elders had invalidated and or rendered ineffective the commandments of God. Consequently, the Lord directly renounced this fatal danger, holding nothing back with the false religious leaders who promoted it.

Here we see that the longer a person has been held captive in man's empty, religious tradition that is devoid of biblical truth, the more that one will fight to maintain it. That is why it is so rare for anyone raised in a tradition of legalism to be open to receive biblical truth. They stubbornly cling to their superficial ways. Because their mind is already made up, they do not want to be confused with the facts. Such a change would require them to admit that they have been wrong for these many years and that their empty tradition has brought them nothing.

In Jesus' day, the Pharisees acknowledged the reality of divine truth in Scripture. But though they claimed to believe it, they, nevertheless, added their own tradition to it. In a short time, their rules and regulations were elevated above the truth. As a result, when Jesus came preaching the pure, unadulterated, divine truth, it created a catastrophic reaction. The infallible words and inspired doctrines that He expounded fueled a dramatic crisis with the leaders of Israel.

By traditions, Jesus meant those man-made rules that were added to the Bible by Israel's religious leaders, requiring everyone's obedience in order to be saved and sanctified. These human regulations were called "the traditions of the elders" and rose to a level of prominence above the divine authority of Scripture. In this elevation, the words of the rabbis became weightier than the words of the prophets. Self-generated religious rules replaced the supreme authority of the Word of God.

This is precisely the crisis that occurred in Mark 7. This critical text addresses the clash between divine truth and human tradition. It records the collision between divine revelation and human rules. It reveals the confrontation between true spirituality and false religion. The more religious and tradition-bound a people are, the more provocatively the truth will be felt. The truth might more easily exist in the context of raw paganism and hedonism than in a legalistic, rule-regulated setting. But any highly-religious people who cling to their man-made religion will always seek to smother out the truth.

To that end, tradition without truth is deadly. It is, quite simply, error grown old. Tradition inevitably digs a rut, and that rut soon becomes a grave in which its adherents are buried. The more staunchly legalistic a religious setting is, the greater will be the conflict when the truth is declared.

Let us now consider this encounter in Mark 7:1-13 between

Jesus and the Pharisees and scribes. It is, in reality, the ongoing clash that continues to this present hour between divine truth and man-devised tradition, when that tradition is a substitute for or is in opposition to the word of God.

The Investigation

This incident begins with two groups of arch foes that Jesus repeatedly faced, specifically the Pharisees and the scribes: "The Pharisees and some of the scribes gathered around Him" (verse 1). If there were ever two groups in human history that clung to their legalistic tradition, it was these two parties. The Pharisees were the most conservative sect in Israel, a strict religious group given to the factitious observance of the Law of God. They were fiercely committed to observing the most minute details of the law. The arch fundamentalists of the day, they believed in the divine inspiration of Scripture, the sovereignty of God, His supernatural activity in the world, and the coming kingdom of God to the earth.

The problem was, however, they added their own man-made rules to the truth. Given enough time, their legalistic additions became tradition that crowded out the truth. Their religious regulations established an external code of religion that entirely bypassed their spiritual inner life. Their self-made religious code never required examining and cultivating their hearts before God. Neither did it require the pursuit of true, inward holiness. Their tradition never called for heart-searching repentance, nor the confession of sin. Their self-styled legal code merely promoted superficial living that gave the appearance of godliness. The Pharisees were absorbed with every minute detail of external righteousness, but neglected any internal relationship observance with God. As their regulations accumulated, still more rules were required to regulate them.

The word "Pharisee" means "separatist." These hyper-

separatistic individuals sought to remove themselves entirely
from the defilements of the world. Their strictness in separation
went so far that they even withdrew themselves from their fel-
low Jews. Instead of going into the world to be a witness for
God, they isolated themselves from people in an effort to cease
from sinning. Due to their rigid adherence to their own religiosity, they became blindly self-righteous. They viewed themselves
genuinely pure before God by the outward observance of their
petty rules. They perceived themselves to be an island of purity
surrounded by an ocean of depravity. These isolationists cut
themselves off from everyone outside their rule-obsessed sect.

We have such Pharisees with us today. They are those religious people who seek to withdraw from the world entirely rather
than reach the world. They spend all their time with only Christians, but never with unbelievers. Some of them will not even
fellowship with other believers whom they consider to be out of
step with their perceptions of what constitutes true spirituality.
Many have so separated themselves from such believers that
they even insist upon a double separation, that is, removing
themselves from those who do not remove themselves from the
world or sin. Simply put, they withdrew from believers who do
not withdraw from others.

The scribes, on the other hand, were not a sect as the Pharisees were, but a profession comprised of lawyers. They studied
the Law of Moses, plus they gave themselves to mastering their
own religious regulations. Many of the scribes were Pharisees
because of their inflexible adherence to the Law. In the Gospels,
we often find the Pharisees and the scribes together, because of
their mutual bent toward legalism. Occasionally, they were
found with the Sadducees, who were the liberals of the day and
denied the strict teaching of the Word. However, the Pharisees
and the scribes were usually found together because both groups
wanted a strict enforcement of the Law of Moses.

The scribes and Pharisees "came from Jerusalem" (verse 1),
which was the headquarters for the religious elite of Israel. The
holy city, Jerusalem, was the religious center of Israel, where the

Temple was built, the Torah was kept, the Sanhedrin presided, and where Jewish traditions thrived. Jerusalem was the hot bed of legalism, the tomb where their dead religion lay. As they "came from Jerusalem," the Pharisees and scribes sought out the Lord Jesus Christ, who was preaching and teaching in Galilee. Their intent was to stop His ministry before it could advance any further. The Sanhedrin, no doubt, had commissioned this group to travel north to the Sea of Galilee, where Jesus was ministering, to discredit Him publicly and put an end to His ministry before it gained any more momentum. As upholders of the traditions of men, these religious leaders were threatened by the truth.

As the Pharisees and the scribes traveled from Jerusalem, they came with great animosity toward Christ. Their hatred would escalate in a concerted effort to have Jesus put to death. His public execution upon the cross will be instigated by these Pharisees and scribes because the truth was too threatening for them.

There were specific reasons why the Pharisees and scribes despised the Lord Jesus Christ. First, Jesus proclaimed the Scripture itself and gave its proper interpretation. This was higher authority than they could claim in their tradition. Second, Jesus claimed to speak from God, the very words that the Father had given to Him. This was an absolute authority that they did not possess. Third, Jesus did not honor their traditions, especially those pertaining to the Sabbath, which infuriated their self-righteous pride. Fourth, Jesus associated with sinners, whom the Pharisees avoided at all costs. Fifth, Jesus exerted great influence over the people, weakening the power base of the Pharisees, while exposing the bankruptcy of their empty traditions. Sixth, Jesus was perfectly holy, which unmasked their religious pretense and sinful hearts. Their means of dealing with Him would be to crucify Him. To be sure, a perfect storm was gathering against the Lord Jesus.

As these religious leaders came to Galilee, it was on a mission to defraud the Lord Jesus. They did not come to sit at His feet, take notes, and be attentive to the things of God. They had no real interest in the truth. Instead, they were there to destroy His ministry before it could spread any further.

Upon their arrival, these religious leaders discovered that they "had seen that some of His disciples were eating their bread with impure hands, that is, unwashed" (verse 2). They spied upon some of His followers and noted that they had not subjected themselves to the ceremonial washings required by their religious rules. The disciples had violated one of their legalistic traditions. They had broken one of their man-made regulations. Something had to be done.

By this time, there was a large number of rules that the Pharisees and scribes had accumulated, so many that the people had difficulty trying to learn and remember them. Worse, who could maintain them? They claimed that in order to be right with God, one must keep all these many laws. Among them were these pertaining to the ceremonial washing of one's hands. After His disciples had been in public contact with sinners, their rules claimed that they must rinse their hands in order to be cleansed from the moral contamination. They had gone into the marketplace where there were unclean Gentiles. In order to step back into a state of acceptance with God, they must go through their ritual of cleansing.

Little has changed today. Those ensnared in legalism today will go to any length to defend their rules and rituals. They will not investigate the truth and then re-examine their confining regulations. Instead, they often persecute the messenger who brings the truth. The more that religious people are tradition-bound in legalism, the more violently they will lash out against the one who speaks the truth. Tradition dies hard, if it ever dies at all. Legalists will attack the messengers of truth at all costs. As it was in the days of Jesus, so it is today. Human nature has not changed over the centuries. This battle against the truth is fought again and again in many churches and religious settings. The truth always generates panic in tradition-bound legalists. Countless pastors and spiritual leaders today preach the truth, and the resulting warfare often costs them their ministry.

The Explanation

The explanation for ceremonial washings is as follows, "For the Pharisees and all the Jews do not eat unless they carefully wash their hands" (verse 3). "All the Jews" indicates a large number practiced this man-made rule. This regulation had nothing to do with the need for the Jews to have sanitary conditions so as not to contract germs. Instead, this practice points to their perceived need to be spiritually cleansed from their daily association with sinners. But observing this tradition was pure religious superstition, having no basis in truth. There were hundreds of such minute stipulations recorded in a book called *The Talmud,* containing these scrupulous Jewish traditions. But keeping them provided no spiritual benefit whatsoever, only harm.

There was another extra-biblical book called *The Mishnah,* which was the compilation of countless Jewish oral laws. The Pharisees and scribes felt that these additional traditions were a fence around the Law that would protect it from passing away. This flawed belief revealed their disregard for the indestructibility of the Word. The Bible had declared, "The grass withers; the flower fades away. But the Word of our God abides forever" (Isaiah 40:8). But despite this clear testimony, they were convinced that the Word of God must be protected and preserved by their many rules.

Their attempt to protect the Law can be seen most clearly in their endless Sabbath regulations. According to their rules, they were forbidden to look into a mirror on the Sabbath because one might find a gray hair and be tempted to pluck it out. Such an act was considered working on the Sabbath. It ever there was straining at a gnat and swallowing a camel, surely this was it! They also said the people were forbidden to wear false teeth on the Sabbath because if they fell out of one's mouth, they would have to pick them up. According to the rabbis, this was considered carrying a burden on the Sabbath.

Moreover, if a person was upstairs on the Sabbath and
wanted to take a handkerchief downstairs, a person would have
to tie it around his or her neck and wear downstairs. But it could
not be carried by hand. Such was considered working on the
Sabbath. Another example concerned a man with a wooden leg,
whose house caught on fire on the Sabbath. A major debate surrounded whether he was allowed to put on his wooden leg in
order to walk out of his house, or was he required to carry it on
the Sabbath in order to flee to safety.

These specific instances represent the mere superficiality with
which their spiritual lives were being conducted. There were
hundreds of these rabbinic rules that required full-time scribes to
oversee their interpretation and application. Over the years, the
list of these hair-splitting rules became increasingly longer and
longer. Apparently the Ten Commandments were not enough to
direct their lives. They were so spiritual, they believed that they
needed more laws to guide them.

As the Pharisees observed the disciples, they "had come from
the marketplace" (verse 4), where a wide cross section of people
had gathered. Among these people were both the religious and
the irreligious. There were Sadducees, zealots, Pharisees, scribes,
Gentiles, merchants, tax collectors, harlots, thieves, robbers, and
more. In such a public setting, they undoubtedly rubbed shoulders with those perceived to be sinners. Thus, the disciples could
not eat a meal unless they first cleansed themselves with a ceremonial washing. If they failed to do so, they were defiled and
unclean before God. Moreover, they were considered to be con-
tagious with the righteous.

A similar confrontation occurred earlier in our Lord's ministry. Matthew 9:10–11 states, "Then it happened that as Jesus was
reclining at the table in the house, behold, many tax collectors
and sinners came and were dining with Jesus and His disciples.
When the Pharisees saw this, they said to His disciples, 'Why is
your Teacher eating with the tax collectors and sinners?'" The
religious leaders of Israel believed that exposure to tax collectors

and notorious sinners would cause one to become morally contaminated. In their minds, Jesus was defiling Himself because he
ate with known sinners. Thus, He must undergo the process of
cleansing Himself through this ritual of hand washing. Clearly,
the Pharisees did not see themselves as sinners.

Another such crisis is found in Matthew 11:19, when the
Pharisees and scribes tried to discredit Jesus, saying: "The Son of
Man came eating and drinking, and they say, 'Behold, a gluttonous man and a drunkard, a friend of tax collectors and sinners!'"
Their charge was that Jesus was eating and drinking with tax collectors and sinners. Worse, they called Him a drunkard and a
gluttonous man because He was spending time with defiled people. Jesus must surely be contaminated with the same sins.

In Luke 15:1–2, we read, "All the tax collectors and the sinners were coming near to Him to listen to Him. The Pharisees
and scribes grumbled, saying 'This man receives sinners and eats
with them.' " In response, Jesus told three parables about a lost
sheep, a lost coin, and a lost son. Jesus gave these stories in order
to explain that He came into this world for this very purpose, to
seek the lost. Therefore, He must spend time with sinners in order to rescue them. But Jesus' association with sinners broke
their rules. It was bad enough that He receives sinners. But that
He eats with them went too far. His hands were contaminated
and His life defiled by this contact. He is eating and drinking
condemnation to Himself, they reasoned, by eating meals with
them.

Sad to say, there are many Christians today who use a similar rational. They believe that they must remain in their "holy
huddle" if they are to remain holy. They are convinced that
there is holiness in a hole. They presume that any contact with
the world renders them impure. So they retreat behind the walls
of their churches and circles of friends, never to engage the world
with the gospel of Christ. Such an isolationist mentality must be
avoided at all costs.

Mark notes: "And there were many other things which they
have received in order to observe, such as the washing of cups

and pictures and copper pots" (verse 4). These "other things" refer to yet further man-made traditions that must be observed. Using eating utensils had minute rules that regulated their supposed proper use. If they gave something to eat to a Gentile, a tax collector, or a known sinner, a Jew would have to cleanse the cup and the pot before they could use it. If not, they would, allegedly, contract the spiritual disease of sinners. This self-righteous attitude drove a wedge between them and everyone else. Such an arrogance bred prejudice in their hearts, causing them to look down at others.

In addition, whenever they entered into the house, they must first clean the eating utensils that known sinners had used before they could use them, lest they become defiled. This is why Jesus would later condemn the Pharisees with His excoriating addresses of "Woe unto you" in Matthew 23. In this rebuke, Jesus condemned the way the Pharisees were conducting themselves. By issuing these woes, Jesus was pronouncing judgment upon them:

> Woe to you, scribes and Pharisees, hypocrites! For you clean the outside of the cup and of the dish, but inside they are full of robbery and self-indulgence. You blind Pharisee, first clean the inside of the cup and of the dish, so that the outside of it may become clean also. (Matthew 23:25–26)

According to their legalistic rules, the Pharisees were ceremonially clean. But this practice entirely neglected the fact that they remained dirty on the inside. These counterfeit regulations cleaned up the outward appearance of their lives. They caused them to look sanctimonious before others. But their hearts were never addressed, nor inwardly cleansed.

Imagine going to someone's house for a meal, and being served a cup that is so clean on the outside it sparkles. But as you put it to your mouth, you notice that on the inside, there is dried milk and a crusted chunk of meat from the last serving.

You would be repulsed. It is more important to clean the inside of the cup than the outside. In like manner, this is how Jesus described the spiritual lives of the Pharisees. They looked so spiritual on the outside. They dressed up well on the Sabbath. They knew how to sound and look religious. But on the inside, Jesus said, they were nothing but dead men's bones.

So it is with all legalism. Man-made rules that go beyond the Scripture can only regulate external matters of behavior. But it can never cleanse sin from the heart. Neither can it sanctify the life. Legalism erects an artificial façade that religious people hide behind, but it never changes the heart of man.

The Confrontation

The Pharisees and scribes confidently stepped forward, convinced that they had an overwhelming case with which they would indict the disciples. The charge was moral impurity by their associations with sinners. "The Pharisees and the scribes asked Him, 'Why do Your disciples not walk according to the tradition of the elders?' " (verse 5). By this inquiring, they were not humble seekers of the truth. They are not asking so that they could be brought into alignment with God's Word. Instead, they posed this question in order to discredit the Lord publicly. The gist of their question is, "Why are You and Your disciples not living under the authority of our tradition? How can You be keeping the Law of God when we provide the right explanation and application of the Law of God? Why do You eat bread with impure hands?"

The hatred in their voices can be distinctly heard in their question. The contempt on their faces could be clearly seen as they policed their rules. They are charging the Holy One of God with breaking their traditions. Certainly, Jesus had posed a threat to their code of conduct that covered up the sin in their evil hearts. The truth is, the Pharisees embraced their rules in order to cover over their corrupt hearts. They attempted to measure true spirituality by their outward appearance, external actions, and their attendance at religious functions. But their hearts were never made clean. No wonder they have targeted Him with this indictment.

Legalism is always like this. It always externalizes spirituality by bypassing the heart. In so doing, it gives the appearance of godliness by striving to be narrower than the truth. But there is no glory in being more confining than the truth. God is honored in observing whatever the truth is, no more no less. The plum line of God's Word does not need to be moved one iota to the left, or to the right. Yet legalism is always departing from the divine standard in order to establish a supposed higher standard for true spirituality. Whenever truth confronts legalism, those who cling to their tradition will be traumatized by the presentation of the Scripture. The more that strictly religious people are imprisoned to their legalistic regulations, the less godly they will be. In such cases, the truth will inevitably provoke people to rise up in anger against it.

In living the Christian life, we must be committed to the Scripture alone. We cannot become entangled with preserving man-made rules that substitute for the Word of God. Divine truth must always take precedence over human tradition. As long as denominations exist, churches meet, and ministries operate, there is an inevitable drift toward legalism in unbiblical traditions. Over time a subtle shift creeps in. Consequently, every attempt must be made to resist whatever opposes the truth.

Legalism can just as easily destroy someone's spirituality as liberalism. This chapter is an urgent call to everyone who finds themselves, as these Pharisees and scribes did, hanging on to their religious rituals and rules as a substitute for true godliness. Genuine Christianity is concerned with a personal relationship with God in the heart. Authentic godliness involves the Word of God being sown into the soul and authentic holiness being produced by the Holy Spirit. True Christianity is entering into fellowship with God through His Son, Jesus Christ. It is not realized by merely being in church, as important as that is. Nor it is by ascribing to a list of man-made rules as a code of conduct. There must be the renouncing of keeping man's empty rules in an attempt to commend one's self to God. Instead, there must be the full reliance of personal faith in Christ that leads to a growing knowledge of Him.

The Condemnation

As this confrontation between the Pharisees and Jesus escalated, the Lord directly condemned their dead religion. He spared no words as He addressed them with the force of a sledgehammer:

> And He said to them, "Rightly did Isaiah prophesy of you hypocrites, as it is written: 'This people honors Me with their lips, But their heart is far away from Me. 'But in vain do they worship Me, Teaching as doctrines the precepts of men.' "Neglecting the commandment of God, you hold to the tradition of men." He was also saying to them, "You are experts at setting aside the commandment of God in order to keep your tradition. "For Moses said, 'Honor your father and your mother'; and, 'He who speaks evil of father or mother, is to be put to death'; but you say, 'If a man says to his father or his mother, whatever I have that would help you is Corban (that is to say, given to God),' you no longer permit him to do anything for his father or his mother; thus invalidating the word of God by your tradition which you have handed down; and you do many things such as that." (Mark 7:6–13)

By these condemning words, the Pharisees and the scribes received far more than they bargained for. Jesus played hardball with these arrogant religious leaders. A point of clarification first needs to be made here. When Jesus spoke to sinners entrapped in this legalistic system, He addressed them with kindness and compassion. Jesus spoke gracious words to those ensnared in the rules of the Pharisees, extending mercy to them. However, to the harsh Pharisees, Jesus held nothing back. A distinction must always be made between the teachers of legalism and those who are ensnared in it.

James 3:1 makes this clear: "Let not many of you become teachers, my brethren, knowing as such we shall incur a stricter judgment." There is a stricter accountability that teachers have before God. The Pharisees and scribes were no exception. How much greater will be their condemnation on the last day. These blind leaders of the blind caused others to become sons of hell. So shall their judgment be much more severe.

Jesus then quoted Isaiah 29:13: "And He said to them, 'Rightly did Isaiah prophesy of you hypocrites' " (verse 6). This word "rightly" means how perfectly or appropriately did Isaiah address the Pharisees and scribes. By this Old Testament citation, Jesus charged them with the same guilt as the false prophets of Israel incurred before them. When Jesus used this inflammatory word, "hypocrites," He charged them with being religious frauds who hid behind a mask of pretense. A hypocrite is one who plays religion, who puts up a front and pretends to be someone other than what he truly is on the inside. Such a person will go to every length to impress others that he is something other than what he is.

Literally, the word "hypocrite" in the Greek language means one who puts on a mask. It was used in the ancient theater to describe a Greek tragedy actor who would go onto a stage, put on a mask, and pretend to be someone that he is not. He would have rehearsed his lines in order to play a part in a play. He would playact, or play a role before an audience. The "hypocrite" would be graded by the onlookers for his performance. A "hypocrite" was like an actor, one who wore a mask and gave a performance. In this case, the word meant one who hid behind a religious façade of external trappings, specifically behind rituals and rules. But such a pretender neglected the inner condition of his own heart.

This was not the first time Jesus had laid this charge at the feet of the Pharisees and scribes. In the Sermon on the Mount, Jesus indicted them with concerning themselves with the mere outward observance of religion, but entirely neglected their own hearts from whence true spirituality flows (Matthew 5:21-48). Jesus said, "So when you give to the poor, do not sound a trumpet before you as the hypocrites do in the synagogues" (Matthew 6:2). By these words, Jesus directed His rebuke against the legalistic system over which the Pharisees presided. In Matthew 7:5, Jesus further said, "You hypocrite, first take the log out of your own eye, and then you will see clearly to take the speck out of your brother's eye." These religious leaders, Jesus said, were blind to their own corruption.

Of all that Jesus had to say to the Pharisees and scribes regarding their hypocrisy, Matthew 23 is the most condemning. In this chapter, Jesus said seven times, "Woe to you scribes and Pharisees, hypocrites" (verses 13, 14, 15, 23, 25, 27, 29). This seven-fold indictment was issued in rapid-fire, staccato fashion. In so many words, Jesus said, "You are blind leaders of the blind. You clean the outside of the cup, but you neglect the inside. You strain at gnats, and you swallow camels. You keep people out of entering into the kingdom of heaven. You tithe out of the herbs that you grow in your backyard. You pluck one tenth of a little tiny leaf, bring it to the Temple, and give it to God. But you completely neglect the weighty matters of the law of justice and mercy and faithfulness."

This religious hypocrisy is precisely what legalism produces. Such false posturing is man's attempt to appear to be what he is not. It is man's efforts to achieve what only God can produce. It is man's fleshly labors to be spiritual by keeping self-fabricated rules. But these stipulations are heavy burdens upon peoples' backs, causing them to be "weary and heavy laden" (Matthew

11:28). Over time, religious leaders added increased regulations until the Scripture was displaced by their own rules.

Having denounced them as hypocrites, Jesus acknowledged that their external appearance was honorable: "This people honors Me with their lips." They talked so piously and sounded so spiritual. They used the right religious vocabulary. They spoke about God. They taught about righteousness. Nevertheless, Jesus said, "but their heart is far away from Me." Their problem was a heart problem. They said one thing, but their heart was something else. He had already confronted this false dichotomy between their lips and their hearts when He said, "Not everyone who says to Me, 'Lord, Lord,' will enter the kingdom of heaven" (Matthew 7:21). In other words, these leaders claim to know the Lord, but, in reality, are outside the kingdom. They are "far away from God," that is, they were separated from Him. They did not know God. An infinite chasm separated them from holy God. When Jesus said, "their heart is far away from Me," He recognized that though they were in a house of worship, their hearts were another world away. They were religious, but lost.

How tragic! There was praise on their lips, but no reality in their hearts. They were mere play actors on the stage of life. When they came into religious services, they were simply rehearsing their lines. They were self-deceived, thinking they were worshiping God, when, in reality, they were nothing more than spiritual fakes. They were religious phonies, who had duped themselves into presuming they were right with God, but they were not. Because they wore a mask, they were unable to see their own hearts.

Jesus said that these religious leaders were "teaching as doctrines the precepts of men." "Teaching" is in the present tense, indicating this was their continual, ongoing activity. They are constantly teaching as doctrines the traditions of men. They espoused what originated in their own minds rather than what God revealed in His Word. Sadly, their religious traditions were keeping them from God.

Jesus boldly charged them with "neglecting the commandment of God" (verse 8). To "neglect" means "to cancel, annul, or abandon." By their legalism, they were annulling the divine commandments. "The commandment of God" comes with divine authority and commands men to obey what it requires. But they neglected the commandment of God in order to "hold to the traditions of the elders." The phrase "hold to" means to take something securely into one's own possession. It means to cling to something tightly, to grasp it with both hands. By saying "you hold to the traditions of men," Jesus meant that they would not relinquish their stranglehold on their traditions. Their petty rules had cancelled the teachings of the Word of God. These pious-sounding leaders had abandoned the truth of God for trivial regulations of men.

Jesus further asserted, "You are experts at setting aside the commandment of God in order to keep your tradition" (verse 9). The word that leaps out of this verse is "experts." Jesus was saying that they were stunningly brilliant at being stupid. They were intellectual geniuses at being fools. They were remarkably good at being bad. They were clever at cancelling God's law. They were adept at annulling the Word. That was the condemnation that Jesus brought against them. With them squarely in view, Jesus had early declared, "Whoever then annuls one of the least of these commandments, and teaches others to do the same, shall be called least in the kingdom of heaven" (Matthew 5:19a). They were "experts" at this.

This warning against setting aside God's Word is needed as much today as when Jesus first uttered it. When divine truth is replaced by human tradition, it keeps people from entering the kingdom of God. Moreover, this attack on the truth invalidates the worship of people. It hinders any growth in godliness. All religious tradition that annuls the Word of God in the lives of people must be confronted. If we are to be blessed, the Word of God *alone* must govern and guide our lives. That was the very heartbeat of the Reformation, *sola Scriptura*, or Scripture alone. Rome said, "Scripture *and* tradition." But Geneva and Zürich and Wittenberg retorted, "Scripture alone." That is the very essence of what Jesus is saying here. The truth of God *and* the tradition of the elders cannot co-exist. They are mutually exclusive, never mutually inclusive. Scripture *alone* must reign over our lives.

The Illustration

Jesus next proceeded to give an illustration of what He was asserting. In verse 10. He no longer remained on the witness chair under their prosecuting attack. Jesus reversed the roles and charged them with violating the Law. In unmistakable terms, Christ brought His plaintive accusation against their bankrupt tradition. A staunch Defender of the truth, Jesus indicted them with annulling the Word of the living God. The specific charge that He brought against them was only one of their many breaches of the Word. In verse 10, Jesus gave this prime example of their breaking the Scripture. Jesus introduced it by saying, "For Moses said." In so doing, Christ did not appeal to one of their rabbis or elders, but cited the authority of Scripture.

By quoting Moses, Jesus affirmed the dual authorship of Scripture. Jesus stated that Moses is the human writer of this passage. However, He subsequently identified that what Moses wrote, in reality, is "the Word of God" (verse 13). Combining these two verses, we see that Jesus affirmed that what Moses wrote is the Word of God. This affirmed His belief in the dual authorship of Scripture, with God being the primary Author and Moses a secondary author, simply the human instrument who recorded it. Though written by the prophet, every jot and tittle in every phrase and word is breathed out of the mouth of God. 2 Timothy 3:16 states: "All Scripture is inspired by God." That means the Bible is "God-breathed," or, literally, breathed out by God. Most correctly, the Scripture is more breathed-out by God, not breathed into by Him. In this process, God used human authors to record His infallible Word. In this instance, the human instrument was Moses, who wrote what God revealed, without error.

Specifically, Jesus cited the fifth commandment of the Decalogue from Exodus 20:12: "Honor your father and your mother" (*cf.* Deuteronomy 5:16). He then quoted Exodus 21:17: "He who speaks evil of father or mother is to be put to death" (*cf.* Leviticus 20:9). A master Teacher, our Lord made a positive assertion first, followed by a negative denial. In this two-fold manner there was no room for any misunderstanding. The Pharisees and the scribes had used their sinister minds to explain away these commandments by looking for loopholes. But Jesus would not allow them to escape its meaning and demands.

Jesus confronted their hypocrisy, rightly using the Law to expose their sinful hearts. The Decalogue clearly commands the honoring of father and mother by every child. Such honor begins with the heart, which, in turn, directs one's words and actions. This command requires that children give the financial support and practical care of one's parents in their latter days. So critically important is this imperative that Exodus 21:17 states that a failure to obey, even speaking evil of one's parents, demands the death penalty. Not giving esteem, courtesy, and support to one's father and mother mandated capital punishment.

Having established the biblical standard, Jesus rebuked them, "But you say, If a man says to his father or his mother, 'Whatever I have that would help you is corban' (that is to say, given to God)" (verse 11). When He said, "But you say," Jesus was quoting their words, which directly contradicted the Scripture. He cited what their tradition espoused, which stood in direct opposition to the teaching of the Word. When Jesus said, "if a man says," He was quoting what they were actually teaching, namely the tradition of the elders.

The word "corban" means'"something given as a gift." In this context it was something given or dedicated to God. Here is how they were experts at invalidating the Word of God. Whenever they came in possession of a vast sum of money, they would immediately consecrate it to God, saying, "God, it is Yours." Then, when their parents became old and needed support financially, the Pharisees were teaching the people to say, "Mom and Dad, I would really like to help you, but I have already committed all my money to God. I wish I could help you. But I have none left over for you." The tradition of the elders taught this so that the people's money would be brought to the Temple in order to support the religious establishment. This way, it was not diverted to help their parents in their need.

Confronting this tradition, Jesus said, "You no longer permit him to do anything for his father or his mother, thus invalidating the Word of God by your tradition which you have handed down; and you do many such things as this" (verses 12–13). The indictment was clear. The Pharisees' man-made rules were turning people away from obeying God's Law, in this instance, from helping their parents. Their tradition was a direct violation of the Word of God. This was certainly not a small matter. As Jesus confronted them with this, the crux of the matter was: Will they follow the truth or their tradition? Will they seek to please God or men? If they hold on to their tradition, they will dishonor God. They must choose.

This is the same choice that every one of us must make. Either we will follow the truth of God's Word or live by the tradition of men. There is no middle ground. There is not a way to straddle this fence and have it both ways. If we follow the truth, it leads to liberty. But if we follow tradition, it leads to the bondage of legalism. It is pride that causes us to cling to man-made rules and regulations for our Christian lives rather than the Scripture. We must repent of all reliance upon human wisdom in order to pursue holiness. Instead, we must obey the commandment of God, which alone leads to life.

The Application

What do we learn from this confrontation between truth and tradition? How should we act upon this? I conclude by giving four action points to help us put this into practice.

First, we must recognize the sufficiency of Scripture. This is a battle line for which we must earnestly contend. We must fight to uphold the truth of the full sufficiency of the Word to do its work in the hearts of people to produce salvation and sanctification. The Scripture is perfect and complete, lacking in nothing. It is able to make one "adequate, equipped for every good work" (2 Timothy 3:17). A believer does not need non-biblical sources to address spiritual issues that pertain to godliness. I hear of churches having a leadership conference, that bring in a well-known figure in the world to address their church officers to be more of what this church needs to be. But a celebrity has nothing to say to the church, no matter how famous he may be, if he does not speak from the Scripture. If this highly-revered individual does not quote Peter and Paul and John, then believers are not helped.

The sufficiency of Scripture is stated in Psalm 19:7 and 9: "The law of the Lord is perfect, restoring the soul. The testimony of the Lord is sure, making wise the simple. The precepts of the Lord are right, rejoicing the heart. The command of the Lord is pure, enlightening the eyes. The fear the Lord is clean, enduring forever. The judgments of the Lord are true. They are righteous all together." This is to say, the Bible is comprehensive and complete, pure and perfect. It revives, refreshes, and renews our souls. There is nothing lacking in it that we need to live the Christian life. Therefore, we must read the Bible, study the Bible, master the Bible, and memorize the Bible. It alone will be used by God for our salvation and our sanctification.

Second, we must resist the hypocrisy of Pharisee-ism. There is a fallen nature within each one of us by which we neglect the inner condition of our own heart. We can easily fall prey to emphasizing the external appearances of our spiritual life to the neglect of the inward purity of our soul. We must resist all attempts to cover over the sin within our hearts. The real person is not our external façade, but what our inner heart is. True spirituality is not found in the outward trappings of our lives. We are what we are in our hearts—no more, no less. Proverbs 4:23

states: "Watch over your heart with all diligence, for from it
flows the springs of life." Our entire spiritual life is flowing from
your heart. Deuteronomy 6:5 commands: "You shall love the
Lord your God with all of your heart and all your soul and all of
your might." Loving God is, first and foremost, a matter of the
heart. 1 Samuel 16:7 explains: "God sees not as man sees, for
man looks on the outward appearance, but God looks upon the
heart." Thus, we must watch over the inner condition of our
soul, our attitudes, and our inner thoughts. As our heart goes, so
goes our entire life.

Third, we must elevate the honor that we have for our parents. This is one of the most important commandments of God.
Obeying this commandment is majoring on majors. This is addressing a primary matter in anyone's life. Honoring our parents
is not a peripheral issue, but one of central importance. If we are
not right with your parents, as much as in us it lies, we are not
right with God. Esteem your father and mother. We must show
love and respect to them. This is what the Apostle Paul says to
all young people. Ephesians 6:1: "Children, obey your parents in
the Lord." This word "obey (ako)," means "to listen up." When
our parents are talking, we should listen to them with undivided
attention. We must consider what our parents are saying to us
and not put them off.

Ephesians 6:1–3 continues: "for this is right. Honor your father and mother (which is the first commandment with a promise), so that it may be well with you and that you may live long
on the earth." Honoring one's parents is so important that God
weighted it with this promise, that good will come to your life.
This is not only for young children, but also for adults, who
should honor their parents by caring for them in the latter years
of their life. Did not Jesus Christ Himself do this as He hung up
on the cross, dying for our sins? Did He not in that moment say,
"Woman, behold your son" (John 19:26)? And did He not say to
the Apostle John, "Behold your mother" (verse 27)? With His
last words, He gave attention to caring for His mother. This example from the cross calls us to give esteem and care to our par-

ents as long as we live.

Fourth, we must see the necessity of the new birth. Entrance into the kingdom of God does not depend upon how religious you are. Jesus said to Nicodemus, the most recognized teacher in Israel in His day, "Except you be born again, you will not see the kingdom of heaven" (John 3:3). External religion cannot give you a new heart. Outward religiosity cannot give you a new life. The tradition of the elders, recorded in man-made rules and regulations, cannot reconcile you to God. Such adherence cannot appease the wrath of God toward your sin. You must be born again. These scribes and Pharisees, who were the most religious people of their day, knew the Word of God and gave themselves to His service. They were constantly in the house of God, and yet they did not know God in their hearts.

Dear reader, have these truths found you out today? Has God removed the mask from your face and allowed you to see your need for a Savior? Are you this moment under the conviction of sin? Do you see that you have need for a new heart and for a new life? The Bible says to you, "Seek the Lord your God. Call upon Him while He is near" (Isaiah 55:6). You will find Him if you search for Him with all of your heart. Jesus said, "Truly, truly, I say to you, he who hears My word, and believes Him who sent Me, has eternal life, and does not come into judgment, but has passed out of death into life" (John 5:24). Commit your soul to Jesus Christ, and you will never stand in judgment for your sin.

If you have never been born again, I urge you this moment to seek God with all of your heart. Humble yourself beneath the mighty hand of God. See that the rags of your self-righteousness will not cover your sin. No amount of religious ritual will ever reconcile you to God. You need a Savior. You need a Mediator to stand between God and you. You need an Advocate to take your case and represent you before God. You need One whose perfect righteousness alone can give you acceptance with God. I urge you this very moment, trust in Jesus Christ.

You do not need to walk an aisle for salvation. That is but

another tradition of the elders. You do not need to talk to a counselor to enter the kingdom. You do not need to repeat a printed prayer that someone else has written for you to merely parrot. What you need to do is to repent of your sins and believe in Jesus Christ. You need to call out to God like the publican and say, "God, be merciful to me, the sinner" (Luke 18:13). If you will turn away from your sin and call upon the name of the Lord, you will find a compassionate and forgiving Savior, who will gather you into His arms and make you one of His own.

That is the truth of God, not a man-made tradition. This truth alone can save you, which no tradition can or will.

Love and God's Law

"If you love Me, you will keep My commandments."
(John 14:15)

Richard D. Phillips

It may seem surprising that in a chapter filled with promises intended by Jesus to comfort His disciples, we also encounter so many uses of the word "if". All through John 14, Jesus does not merely tell us of His provision for the disciples during His absence from earth, but He also tells the conditions by which we may be certain of these promises. In verse 3 Jesus said, "If I go and prepare a place for you, I will come again and will take you to myself." Here, Christ's return to gather us into glory is conditioned on His first departing from earth in his ascension. In verse 9 Jesus answered Thomas, "If you had known Me, you would have known My Father also." Knowing Jesus is the required condition for knowledge of God the Father; we can experience the latter only if we possess the former. Likewise, in verse 14, Jesus conditions His actions on our behalf with the "if" of prayer: "If you ask Me anything in My name, I will do it."

The "ifs" of John 14 do not make our salvation less certain, but more certain, provided the conditions are met. Christians must comprehend Christ, and then we will understand God. Christians must pray, and then Christ will answer. These are cause and effect relationships in God's economy on which we may be absolutely certain, and from which we may derive great comfort. Particularly important among this list of "if" conditions is one that pertains to our love for Christ. In this case, the result of our love for Jesus is as certain as it is important: "If you love Me, you will keep My commandments" (John 14:15).

Love and the Law

Many people, including some Christians, have difficulty

thinking of love and obedience together; we may act either in love or in law, but not both. Among liberals, who are willing to dismiss the Bible's teaching, it is often said that what matters is not law, but only love. On this basis, recent generations have been taught a "new morality" in which the only guideline is love. Anything is permissible so long as it does not seem to hurt anyone. This has been the driving idea behind the "situational ethics" approach that now dominates contemporary society. Its originator, Joseph Fletcher, said, "Only love is a constant; everything else is a variable."[1] Under this thinking marriages may be casually dissolved, adultery may be celebrated, contracts may be broken, parents may be disregarded, and worldly things may be coveted, and all is justified on the grounds that no one was hurt and that love was the motive.

There are two major problems with this view, however. The first is that we must ask how to define love. In the new morality, love is generally defined according to the 1960's philosophy of Jerry Rubin: "If it feels good, do it." But, as the drug culture of the '60's proved, there are things that feel good that are not loving, but that destroy the person who does them and others. The Bible says that the heart is "deceitful above all things" (Jeremiah 17:9), so in reality we cannot trust our own feelings as a guide to love. Thus a young man who seduces a woman into sexual sin is not loving her, however good it may feel at the time. Likewise, a young woman who tempts men into lust by her immodest way of dressing is not loving her neighbor, however good the attention may feel to her at the time.

This raises a question: Has God provided us with an objective guide to love? The answer is Yes, God has done this very thing in His law. Jesus summarized God's law in terms of love. The first great commandment, He said, is to "love the Lord your God

---

[1] Cited by Peter Barnes, in The Presbyterian Church of Victoria, *Love Rules: The Ten Commandments for the 21st Century* (Edinburgh: Banner of Truth, 2004), 9.

with all your heart and with all your soul and with all your mind." The second great commandment is to "love your neighbor as yourself" (Matthew 22:37–39). This division corresponds to the two halves of the Ten Commandments, the first half of which pertains to love for God and the second half to love for our neighbor. The way to love one another, then, is to observe the commandments, not only in their prohibitions, but also in terms of their positive agenda. We not only do not murder, but we protect; we not only do not steal, but we provide. Compared to God's law of love, the "new morality" is revealed as justifying a self-love that does indeed hurt other people.

This leads to a second problem with the "new morality" of love, namely that it utterly excludes the value of love for God. According to Jesus, this is the very first priority, so we must not have a view of love that conflicts with God's definition and standards of love.

Our society asks, for instance, what is wrong with a few harmless lies? The first answer is that it shows no love for God, who is a God of truth and hates lying lips (Proverbs 6:16–17). The second answer is that we are not loving our neighbor when we speak falsely and deceive. For these reasons, the antinomianism of liberal theology (antinomianism combines the words "against" and "law" to become "against law") is not in fact an ethics of love, and its prevalence in our society in recent decades has brought misery and ruin to millions of people.

There is, however, an antinomianism of another kind among Bible-believing Christians, namely those who conceive a radical contrast between law and grace in such a way that Christians are no longer to obey God's law. This can be seen among some Dispensationalists, who tend to see the Old and New Testaments as teaching different approaches to God and salvation, and by Lutherans, who tend to react against law-keeping out of concern for legalism. Noting that the Ten Commandments are part of the Old Testament, and also noting that we are justified through faith alone in Christ, who kept the law for us, these Christians will assert that we are therefore saved in such as way as to be free from obedience to God's law. All we need for salvation is to trust and love the Lord Jesus Christ.

The first problem with this Christian antinomianism is that the New Testament strongly emphasizes the Christian's duty to obey God's law. Paul writes that while we are saved from our failure to keep God's law, we are justified through faith in Christ "in order that the righteous requirement of the law might be fulfilled in us," as we walk in the power of God's Holy Spirit (Romans 8:4).

The second problem with the view that we need only love, but not obey, is Jesus' own teaching on love for Him: "If you love Me, you will keep My commandments" (John 14:15). According to Jesus, the Christian's bond of love with Jesus does not free us *from* keeping God's law, but frees us *to* keeping His commandments. If we love Jesus, that love will draw us to thoughts and actions that conform with Jesus' thoughts and actions, and please Him. William Barclay comments: "It was by His obedience that Jesus showed His love to God; and it is by our obedience that we must show our love to Jesus."[2]

Loving and Obeying Jesus

John 14:15 makes a number of important points about Christian obedience. The first is that our obedience to Christ's commands is *personal* obedience. That is, we do not obey a cold legal code, but we offer obedience to Jesus Himself. He calls us to obey "My commands." This shows the divine lordship of Jesus Christ. Moses never called Israel to obey "my commands," but Jesus unreservedly calls us to personal obedience out of love for Him. Charles Spurgeon wrote: "There are some men for whom you would do anything; you will to yield to their will. If such a

---

[2] William Barclay, *The Gospel of John,* 2 vols. (Philadelphia: Westminster, 1975), 2:193.

person were to say to you, 'Do this,' you would do it without question. Perhaps he stands to you in the relation of a master, and you are his willing servant. Perhaps he is a venerated friend, and because you esteem and love him, his word is law to you. The Savior may much more safely than any other be installed in such a position."[3] Both in His person as the perfect Son of God and in His work, having shown us the highest love by dying for our sins, Jesus has earned the right to call us to personal obedience: "If you love Me, you will obey My commands."

Second, we note in Jesus' words the intimate connection between love for and obedience to him. The only kind of true obedience to the Lord is *loving* obedience. That is, we must obey Christ's commands willingly, gladly, and freely, as an intentional expression of our thanks and love to Him. Spurgeon comments: "The essence of obedience lies in the hearty love which prompts the deed rather than in the deed itself... Love is the chief jewel in the bracelet of obedience."[4] How dead and useless is obedience to the letter of God's law without love to Christ! As Paul said, "If I give away all I have, and if I deliver up my body to be burned, but have not love, I gain nothing" (1 Corinthians 13:3). We see this in those who obey the letter of Sabbath observance, but never rest their hearts in Jesus on the Lord's Day. We see it again in those who are careful to tithe, but take no delight in giving to the gospel work of Christ's church. We could say the same about sexual purity, obedience to marital duties, church membership vows, and many other matters. Obedience to the Bible is only obedience to Christ when given out of love for Him.

Third, Jesus teaches the *certainty* of obedience where there is love for Him. It is important to note that John 14:15 does not express a command, as it is rendered by the King James Version: "If you love Me, keep My commands." Jesus uses the future

---

[3] Charles Haddon Spurgeon, *The Metropolitan Tabernacle Pulpit*, 63 vols. (Pasadena, TX: Pilgrim, 1974), 32:653.
[4] Ibid., 32:652-653.

tense rather than the imperative, pointing out that "if you love Me, you *will* keep My commands." A desire to walk in His way and embrace His teaching is the inevitable result of loving Christ. Indeed, it is *only* love that will motivate us to keep Christ's commands, since to do so we must, like Him, take up the cross, crucifying our love of self so as to love the Lord and love one another as He has loved us. This means that the key to obeying Christ is to cultivate a love for Him, which comes from reflecting on His love for us. John wrote in his first epistle: "We love because He first loved us" (1 John 4:19). This love for Christ will necessarily and inevitably result in a desire to obey His commands.

How We Know We Love Jesus

Jesus' teaching plainly shows how essential it is that believers should love Him. Spurgeon writes: "He that believes in the Lord Jesus Christ for his salvation produces as the first fruit of his faith love to Christ; this must be in us and abound, or nothing is right."[5] This priority is confirmed in the New Testament. What was it that Jesus asked Peter when He restored him to discipleship? Since Peter fell away before the cross, did Jesus ask, "Peter, do you now understand the doctrine of the atonement?" Understanding doctrine is essential, especially when it comes to the meaning of Christ's death, but that is not what Jesus asked Peter. Nor did Jesus ask of his plans for spiritual improvement: "Peter, have you taken steps to make sure this problem doesn't arise again?" What did Jesus ask Peter? He asked, "Simon, son of John, do you love Me?" (John 21:16).

This raises the important question: "How do we know that we love Jesus?" The answer is found in our verse, which we may reverse to say, "We know that we love Jesus if we keep His com-

---

[5] Ibid., 32:653.

mands." This is how Jesus puts it in verse 21: "Whoever has My commandments and keeps them, he it is who loves Me."

To what, then, is Jesus specifically referring when He speaks of His commands? To answer, we should note how Jesus touches on this same matter throughout this chapter. In verse 21, Jesus speaks again of His "commandments," but in verses 23 and 24 He expands His meaning to include His whole teaching: "If anyone loves Me, he will keep My word....Whoever does not love Me does not keep My words." Thus we must understand Jesus' commands to embrace all His teaching, whether it is doctrinal or ethical. Indeed, when we realize that the New Testament apostles spoke for Jesus and that the Old Testaments prophets were servants of Christ's covenant, we rightly expand Jesus' commands to embrace the whole of the Bible. A. W. Pink explains: "The whole revelation of the Divine will, respecting what I am to believe and feel and do and suffer, contained in the Holy Scriptures is the law of Christ....The commandments of Christ include whatever is good and whatever God hath required of us."[6] There is no division between the will of Christ and the will of God, so the Word of God is the Word of Christ. This does not mean that we do not love Jesus unless we are obeying perfectly every line in the Bible. Rather, a love for Christ will instill in us a loving, obedient, and willing attitude towards all that is taught in God's Word. The Bible will become God's Word for us and we will love it as that which both leads us to Christ and teaches us how to obey the commands of our dearly beloved Lord.

Does this mean, therefore, that if we find ourselves struggling with sin, or if we find it difficult to obey God's Word, that we therefore must have no love for Jesus? The answer is No: a struggle to obey does not rule out love for Christ. We all struggle with sin, as John emphasized in his first epistle (1 John 1:8), because we all are still sinners and must contend with our sinful

---

[6] Arthur W. Pink, *Exposition of the Gospel of John* (Grand Rapids: Zondervan, 1975), 776.

nature. But if we love Jesus, we *will* struggle and not give ourselves over to sin. This means that if you are a teenager, you may sometimes think your parents are hopelessly ignorant, but because you love Jesus you will nonetheless seek to obey and respect your father and mother. If you are a husband, your sinful flesh may desire to neglect your wife at the expense of your hobbies or career ambitions but, loving Jesus, you will turn your heart to your wife and children so as to be faithful servant of the Lord. Similarly, Christian wives may sometimes resent the Bible's teaching to submit to their husbands and will grow weary of expending themselves in ceaseless service to their families. They may look out the window at other women who are living for themselves to the detriment of their husbands and children, and feel a twinge of envy, but, because they love Jesus, Christian women will turn back to their husbands with respect and to their families with devotion, doing it all "as to the Lord" (Ephesians 5:22).

Struggling with sin does not mean that we do not love Jesus; if we love Jesus, we will struggle and we will seek Christ's power in prayer that we might obey His commands. The good news is that those who love Jesus will be helped by the mighty Holy Spirit whom Jesus will send. As Jesus continues in John 14:16: "I will ask the Father, and He will give you another Helper to be with you forever." Loving Jesus, we are not left to obey Him in our own small strength, but He gives us His strength from heaven through the ministry of the Spirit, so that our love for Him is enabled to express itself in obedience to His commands.

Having noted that Jesus' commands must be seen as encompassing the whole Bible, we should still note His special emphasis on our love for one another. Jesus earlier taught: "A new commandment I give to you, that you love one another; just as I have loved you, you also are to love one another" (John 13:34). Later, Jesus repeats this special command: "This is My commandment, that you love one another as I have loved you. Greater love has no one than this, that someone lay down his life for his friends" (John 15:12–13).

With this in mind, love for Jesus is certain to yield obedience to Him in the form of *service to others*. We remember how Jesus began His teaching at this last gathering of His disciples prior to the cross by taking up the servant's towel and washing the disciples' feet. Jesus said, "You call Me Teacher and Lord, and you are right, for so I am. If I then, your Lord and Teacher, have washed your feet, you also ought to wash one another's feet" (John 13:13–14). James Boice comments: "This is the picture Jesus gave of true Christianity. It is the attitude that divests itself of its own prerogatives in order to serve others."[7]

Moreover, our love for Jesus will produce an obedience that involves *sacrifice*. "This means that we are not called to serve only when we can do so conveniently and at no cost to ourselves. It means that we are called to serve at our cost when we would much rather do something else."[8] In other words, our love for one another in Christ's name is modeled on His sacrificial love for us. "Love one another as I have loved you," He said (John 15:12), and Jesus loved us by offering His life for our sake on the cross.

Finally, the love for others that reflects Christ's love will involve *sharing*. We are to share ourselves with others, freely giving of our time, talents, and spiritual gifts. We are to share the provision God has given to us so that others might have their needs provided for. Most importantly, the love of Jesus calls us to share the good news of salvation through faith in Him, so that others may know and love Jesus Christ and find eternal life in Him. Here, the command to love merges with the last of Jesus' commandments, given just before He ascended into heaven: "Go into all the world and proclaim the gospel to the whole creation" (Mark 16:15). How can we claim to love Christ if we neglect this great command to share His love with others?

---

[7] James Montgomery Boice, *The Gospel of John*, 5 vols. (Grand Rapids: Baker, 1999), 4:1109.
[8] Ibid.

Love, Obedience, and Assurance

We should conclude our study of this important verse by considering the relationship between love, obedience, and our assurance of salvation. This is important because love for Christ is integral to our faith in Christ, and it is only through faith in Christ that we are saved. Because this is so important, in his first epistle John made explicit the link between our love for Jesus, our obedience to Jesus' commands, and our assurance of salvation: "By this we know that we have come to know Him, if we keep His commandments.... Whoever keeps His word, in him truly the love of God is perfected. By this we may be sure that we are in Him" (1 John 2:3, 5). John does not say that we are saved by obeying Christ's commands, since salvation is by faith alone, but rather that we *know we are saved* only through a love for Christ that obeys His Word.

This teaching makes two vital statements concerning our assurance of salvation. First, if we have no motivation to obey Jesus Christ and thus are not living a life of increasing obedience to His Word, we should have serious concerns about our salvation. To trust Christ is always to love Christ, and he adds: "If you love Me, you will obey My commands."

Merely professing faith in Jesus, without bearing the fruit of that faith in obedience, provides no grounds for the assurance of salvation. In the Sermon on the Mount, Jesus spoke to those who practiced religion, but did not obey Him in love: "I never knew you; depart from Me, you workers of lawlessness" (Matthew 7:23). He explained: "Not everyone who says to Me, 'Lord, Lord,' will enter the kingdom of heaven, but the one who does the will of My Father who is in heaven" (Matthew 7:21). This was not to establish a works basis for salvation, but rather to point out that a saving love for Jesus will always yield the fruit of a life of obedience to His commands. Therefore, if you have professed faith in Christ, but have neither made progress in biblical obedience nor gained a desire to do so, you should reconsider what you mean by faith in Christ. Biblical faith is never a bare assent to beliefs, but always includes a trust in Christ that yields a personal commitment and surrender to His holy will. If you have not offered yourself wholeheartedly to Christ, then you are not saved, and He calls you to a true faith, trusting in His love, that will yield salvation.

Second, if you love Christ and sincerely desire to honor Him through obedience to His Word, this can only be because you are born again to a new and eternal life in Jesus. This is the point of John's teaching in his first epistle—not to cause true believers to doubt their salvation, but to encourage weak and faltering believers to have assurance through the evidence of their faith. Even if your obedience is flawed and incomplete, do you find yourself desiring to change in a Christ-like direction? How can this be if you are not a true believer? Do you not realize that it is mankind's nature, apart from Christ, to rebel against God and resent His commands? Paul writes: "The mind that is set on the flesh is hostile to God, for it does not submit to God's law; indeed, it cannot" (Romans 8:7). How is it, then, that you are not hostile to God's law, but that you desire to show your love to Christ by obeying Him, that you are frustrated by your failure to obey God's law, and that you are in fact increasingly finding that you do keep God's law and find great joy in doing so? The only reasonable answer is that you must be a Christian. James Boice explains: "When a man or woman begins to obey God, first in responding to His offer of salvation in the Lord Jesus Christ, and then in a growing desire to live a Christ-like life, this is evidence of a divine and supernatural working in his or her life. It is proof that God is present and that He has already began a regenerative work within the individual."[9]

Be greatly encouraged, then, if you desire to show your love to Jesus by obeying His commands. Take heart, and be assured of God's saving work in your life. Now press on in new obedi-

---

[9] Ibid., 4:1108.

ence, and enter into the joy of yielding yourself more and more fully in loving embrace of Christ's commands, knowing that in this way you not only prove your love of Christ to yourself, but you show your love to Him who has loved you and laid down His life for your sins.

The Cross Is Enough
Bruce Bickel

Many well-meaning Christians live their lives like children on a playground. They go from toy to toy, from the swing to the merry-go-round, and then to the slide. Many believers go from seminar to seminar, to videos to the latest spiritual offering designed to improve their relationship to God. Several years ago it was spiritually fashionable to wear the bracelet inscribed with the initials "WWJD", meaning "What would Jesus do?" Honestly, many times I have no idea what Jesus would do in a given situation, but the one thing I am absolutely sure of is "WHJD"— *What Has Jesus Done*? One may say this is trivial and not a critical issue. What's the difference? Thinking WWJD can help a person become more Christ-like, can't it, they might say. Granted, there is some validity to that, but behind it lurks the subtle attitude of thinking that the justifying and completed work of the Lord Jesus Christ on the cross must be supplemented by one's own works in order to deepen one's relationship to God.

That is laying the foundation for legalism. Legalism results in the unbiblical emphasis upon works in the matter of justification, God's declaration that a person is legally righteous because all of the Law's claims regarding him are satisfied. Legalism is not the act itself, but rather the motive behind the act. For instance, providing an act of mercy can be a legalistic deed or a God-pleasing act of worship—the difference lies in the motive.

That's why legalism is so subtle. It is the attitude, motive, or intention that leads someone to try to establish, maintain, or improve a righteous standing before God by one's own efforts or activities. It's a refutation of the sufficiency of Christ by assuming that the saving work He accomplished for His people is insufficient and we must do things to improve our legal standing before God by adding to what Christ has done. The legalist thinks that he or she can earn more of God's favor and that they are more acceptable to Him because of their performance. Subtly it says that I have secured something in addition to what Christ has done for me (WHJD). Legalism is an attack on justification by faith alone through grace alone in Christ alone.

Understanding the implication of justification by faith alone is paramount to the maturation of any follower of Christ and is a defense against legalism. The justified sinner cannot be any more righteous in the sight of God or the court of heaven than he is at the moment of his salvation. Because of the person and work of Christ—His sinless perfection and perfect obedience—the Lamb of God became the acceptable sacrifice to pay for sin (2 Corinthians 5:21). The newest believer who has been justified by grace through faith in Christ is at that moment of first belief as righteous as he or she ever can be. That person is forgiven of all sins (because they are imputed, that is, credited to Christ) and wrapped with the flawless righteousness of Christ (because it is imputed, credited, to the believer). We can never add to that perfect righteousness, yet legalism tries to do just that.

There is a story about Napoleon Bonaparte that illustrates this. His personal mount broke free of the corral and ran away. A private in the French army ran after the horse, retrieved it, and brought it back to the general. He handed the reins to Napoleon who took them in his hands, looked at the young private and said, "Thank you, Captain." The young man never doubted the word of his commander. He immediately went to the quartermaster, exchanged his uniform for those of a captain, removed his gear from his tent, and took up residency in the officer's quarters. There was an immediate transformation of his standing in the army. Such is the immediacy of the change of legal position before God by grace alone through Christ alone in justification—a justified sinner cannot become more righteous than what God declares him to be at the moment God declares it. There is no condemnation for those who are in Christ Jesus (Romans 8:1).

Someone might object to what was just said as follows: "Aren't we as Christians to obey God's Law and do good works?" Of course we are, but the legalist regards obedience as a condition for achieving God's grace while the Christian with the right motive regards obedience as a response to receiving God's grace. Dr. D. Martyn Lloyd-Jones, the renowned English preacher of several decades ago stated, "If the 'grace' you have received does not help you to keep the law, you have not received grace."

Jesus said, "If you love Me, you will keep My commandments" (John 14:15 ESV). Grace does not make obedience optional. While God has removed good works as a condition for His acceptance, He has not removed righteousness as a requirement for life. God saves people so they will obey Christ (1 Peter 1:2).

Consider the prophecy of Jeremiah declaring that New Covenant obedience will be greater than Old Covenant obedience (Jeremiah 31:31–34). God's implanting His laws within His people and writing His laws upon their hearts can be seen also in Ezekiel 36:22–27, specifically verses 25–27:

> I will sprinkle clean water on you, and you shall be clean from all your uncleannesses, and from all your idols I will cleanse you. And I will give you a new heart, and a new spirit I will put within you.

> And I will remove the heart of stone from your flesh
> and give you a heart of flesh. And I will put my
> Spirit within you, and cause you to walk in my stat-
> utes and be careful to obey my rules (ESV).

The purpose for this act of grace is revealed in verse 23: "And the nations will know that I am the Lord, declares the Lord God, when through you I will vindicate my holiness before their eyes."

God never requires of us something He doesn't equip us to do beforehand. We are the means by which the world will see that He is holy. So how does He equip us to fulfill our purpose in life? Notice the following sequence: He calls us to Himself— election (v.24). He cleanses us from ourselves—redemption (v.25). He creates a new life within us—regeneration (v.26). He completes us with a new source of power—the Holy Spirit (v.27a). And He causes us to be obedient (v.27b). God takes responsibility for our obedience by equipping us to walk in His statues and obey His rules. Obedience is how we fulfill our life's purpose, and God has equipped us, by grace, to do so.

God cares about what we do. Licentiousness says God does not care what we do; legalism says God approves of you based upon what you do; grace says God accepts you because of what Christ did for you (WHJD). God does not love us more because we obey Him, but we cannot know the blessings of His love without obedience. Thus, a grace focus that undermines Christ's own demand for obedience denies us both the knowledge of and the joy of intimacy with Him. Focusing on what Jesus has done for us at the cross produces a love response in obedience and removes the tendency to strive to please Him for our own benefit. Resting on God's grace does not relieve us of our holy obligations; rather it equips us to fulfill them.

Paul's comparison of Old Covenant obedience and New Covenant obedience is quite graphic. The contrast in the two arrangements, Paul says, is one of permanence (See 2 Corinthians 3:7–18). Essentially, in comparing the two, Paul says that obedience that comes from us fades and obedience that comes from God lasts. Both arrangements come from God so both are glorious. The major difficulty of the Old Covenant was that it made God's favor dependent upon people's obedience: "If you obey, I will be your God" (Ezekiel 11:19–20). The major remedy of the New Covenant is that God provides the obedience (Jeremiah 31:31–34). The gospel of grace is more glorious because the old arrangement was external and fading, radiant on Moses' face; the gospel is internal and permanent (see again Ezekiel 36:22–27). The reason that it is permanent is because it is administered to people solely by the mediation and merit of Christ, who alone, as the incarnate Son, has perfectly obeyed God's holy law. Obedience is essential in both arrangements, but the "If you obey" is changed to "I will put My law in their minds, write it on their hearts, and they will follow Me." The Old demanded obedience, but could not secure it. In the New, God causes us to walk in obedience because He has changed the disposition and motive of the heart through regeneration, that is, being born from above.

Because obedience in the New Covenant is not the condition of the arrangement and free grace has taken its place, many tend to abuse grace either by being antinomian (anti-law: obedience is not necessary) or legalistic (there is merit in my obedience). Many well-intended, Bible believing, conservative church members succumb to the subtlety of legalism by relying partly upon their sanctification to make a contribution to their justification.

The remedy for legalism is to focus on the accomplishments of the Lord Jesus Christ at Calvary, to comprehend more fully WHJD.

The "Good News" is not only what happened inside us at our rebirth, but also what happened for us over 2000 years ago. Our faith is in what He accomplished for us and inside us; we have been given a heart that believes (relies upon, trusts in, depends upon, and adheres to) that. Hebrews 8:6–7 states that "Christ has obtained a ministry that is as much more excellent than the old as the covenant He mediates is better, since it is enacted on better promises." Christ guarantees the terms of the new arrangement because He has already obtained them. So our faith is in what has already been obtained by the One who has obtained it, faith in what God has done. The cross is enough.

Sources cited and/or referred to for further study:

The Bible Exposition Commentary. Warren Wiersbe/
Scripture Press Publications
Are You Legalistic? Robert G. Spinney/Tulip Books
Holiness by Grace: Bryan Chapell/ Crossway Books
Essential Truths of the Christian Faith: R. C. Sproul/
Tyndale House Publications
Romans 5-8: Martyn Lloyd-Jones/Zondervan

The Danger of Legalism
Galatians 4:8–11
Steven J. Lawson

However at that time, when you did not know God, you were slaves to those which by nature are no gods. But now that you have come to know God, or rather to be known by God, how is it that you turn back again to the weak and worthless elemental things, to which you desire to be enslaved all over again? You observe days and months and seasons and years. I fear for you, that perhaps I have labored over you in vain (Galatians 4:8–11).

These are passionate words from the Apostle Paul as he pours out his heart to the Galatians. He is fearful that for all his sacrifice, travel, teaching, and preaching they have received the Word of God in vain. He is concerned that his pastoral labor has had no lasting effect in their spiritual lives. This apprehension is the result of the fatal legalism that was spreading like a deadly cancer throughout their church body. Such a false pursuit of Christian living can leave a pastor wringing his hands and feeling that his entire ministry with those whom he shepherds is of no effect. Such was the threatening reality Paul faced.

Legalism always poses a great danger because it is a dramatic departure from the Word of God. There are two main strands of legalism that must be avoided at all costs. One is the legalism that attacks justification, and the other is that which assaults sanctification. The first damns the souls of unbelievers; the latter destroys the spirituality of believers. Both versions must be refuted and refused.

As it concerns justification, legalism adds false requirements for salvation to faith alone in Christ alone. This brand of legalism says you must believe in Christ *and* perform good works in order to be saved. It claims you must trust Christ *and* be baptized in order to be right with God. Or you must receive Christ *and* be a good person *and* participate in certain religious activities in order to achieve acceptance with God. It is a religion of "and." There is no end to what is required to be added to justification by faith. With legalism, a person must do this and that in order to be right with God. But whatever good works are performed, it can never be enough for one to be received by God. People who have bought into this false gospel lay on their deathbed and call for a religious leader to come to administer last rites because they still have not done enough to be saved. They have water sprinkled on them so that somehow they will be pushed into the kingdom as they die. Yet they remain outside the kingdom of God, if that is their trust.

Such legalism corrupts the true, saving gospel of Jesus Christ, turning it into a false, non-saving gospel, that is no gospel at all. Legalism drives a stake into the very heart of the gospel. It is a total departure from the saving grace of God. That is why the Apostle Paul was so adamant in saying, "If any man is preaching another gospel contrary to what you received, he is accursed" (Galatians 1:9). By this, Paul declared that anyone who preaches a legalistic gospel should go to hell now before he deceives others into the flames below with his false teaching. That is legalism as it relates to justification. It is adding anything to salvation by grace alone, through faith alone, in Christ alone. With unmistakable clarity, Paul speaks in the first three chapters of Galatians that justification is by faith alone, period, paragraph, end of discussion.

As we look at Galatians 4:8–11, Paul is tackling a legalism of a different nature. It is not legalism that blocks entrance into the kingdom by corrupting the teaching of justification by faith alone. Rather, it is the legalism that attacks sanctification and spiritual growth into Christ-likeness. It is the second version of the legalism mentioned earlier, namely that once one is justified he or she lives by a set of man-made rules to achieve true spirituality. Such legalism says that the Bible is not enough and that an additional list of regulations must be followed that govern one's external behavior. Under this guise, spiritual leaders have added to what the Scripture states with a compilation of "do's" and "don'ts" not found in Scripture. An artificial standard for godliness to which one must adhere is erected. This is precisely what Paul has in his mind as he writes these verses in Galatians 4. The apostle is addressing those in the Galatian churches who have succumbed to the fatal danger of legalism that externalizes spirituality and neglects the heart.

Specifically, the legalism addressed here was that which sought to put a believer back under the Old Testament ceremonial law in order to be spiritual. To be righteous, it claimed, one must keep what was required in the Mosaic ceremonial law. That is specifically what Paul is referring to in verses 9 and 10. They must observe Old Covenant "days" (festival days) and "months" (certain seasons that the Old Testament prescribed, such as Passovers and the Feast of Tabernacles) and "years" (sabbatical years and jubilee years) in order to advance in godliness. But these observances, Paul asserts, cannot help one grow as a Christian. In fact, they have the very opposite effect, actually impeding spiritual progress. Such legalism always enslaves and paralyzes its adherents in their sanctification, thus, restricting their growth into spiritual maturity.

Such legalism today must be resisted like a plague. There is no church more spiritually immature than one that is legalistic. No believers are more stunted in their spiritual advancement than those who adopt a strict list for acceptable spiritual behavior that goes beyond what Scripture prescribes. Such an approach to sanctification ensnares people. It retards them because they think that they are actually mature because they do or do not do certain things. The apostle understands what they do not discern, how this legalism is causing them to remain spiritual babes, hindering their advance into adulthood. So Paul in these few verses must confront them with the danger of their legalism.

There are three main headings in verses 8 through 11 that will guide our approach. In verse 8, we will see their past bondage in sin; at the beginning of verse 9, we see their powerful conversion to Christ; in the middle of verse 9 through 11, we see their present drift toward legalism.

Their Past Bondage in Sin

Paul begins this brief section by reminding the Galatians what they once were before they came to Christ: "However, at that time, when you did not know God" (verse 8). This looks back to their spiritual condition before their conversion to Christ. "That time" refers to their unconverted days before coming to faith in Christ. At "that time," they did not know God in a personal, saving way. They were ignorant of God, without the saving knowledge of Christ.

Certainly, there was a certain knowledge the Galatians had *about* God before they were believers. Every unconverted person, whether they have grown up in the church or out of it, has a degree of knowledge *about* God. There is a common knowledge *about* His existence and His attributes that come from general revelation in creation (Psalm 19:1; Romans 1:19–20). There is also a divine knowledge *about* God that comes from the law of God that is written upon every man's heart, known as the law of conscience (Romans 2:14–15). All those who are without Christ are described as "Being darkened in their understanding, excluded from the life of God because of the ignorance that is in them, because of the hardness of their heart" (Ephesians 4:18).That is, all unbelievers are ignorant of God. Their true understanding of Him is darkened. Their hearts are hardened in unbelief.

Occasionally, when I hear someone give their testimony, they will say, "I have always known God." But no one has always known Him. All people were born ignorant of God. All persons enter this world in spiritual darkness, separated from God. Everyone joins the human race without the knowledge of God. There is no true knowledge of God outside of knowing the Lord Jesus Christ.

At "that time," Paul continues, "you were slaves to those which by nature are no gods" (verse 8). When one does not know God, he or she is enslaved to "no gods" of their own fallen imagination. This is the inevitable result of not knowing God. These people have concocted vain ideas about a deity. They have given names to these non-existent gods, created myths about them, and assigned them imaginary wives and children. They have built temples in order to bring them incense. They lift up their blasphemous names and make sacrifices to them. They try to please them and secure their favor. But such deities are nothing but the vain speculations of the darkened minds of men. These "no gods" exist only in their empty, religious superstitions. In reality, these "no gods" are just that, no gods; they are nothing at all.

That they were once "enslaved" to their false deities means that their entire being was previously in bondage to their sin and to the demands of these non-existent gods. Their minds were enslaved to wicked thoughts. They were held captive by the lusts of their sinful flesh. They were imprisoned by the bondage of their perverse wills. Jesus said, "Everyone who commits sin is the slave of sin" (John 8:34). That is, everyone who lives a lifestyle of sin does so because they are under the tyranny of their cruel master, sin. They once pursued and practiced sin because they were slaves of sin, obeying this wicked master.

Paul affirms this elsewhere. To the Romans, he writes: "You are slaves of the one whom you obey, either of sin resulting in death or of obedience resulting in righteousness" (Romans 6:16). This means that every unbeliever is the slave of sin. All people are a slave, either of Christ or of sin. No one is without a master. There is no middle ground. "No man can serve two masters" (Matthew 6:24). If sin is one's master, as with every unbeliever, then one will obey and serve sin. If Christ is one's master, as with every true believer, then one will obey and follow Him. It is an "either/or," not a "both/and."

Peter stated the same: "They themselves are slaves of corruption; for what a man is overcome, by this he is enslaved" (2 Peter 2:19). This is to say, every unconverted person is enslaved to the corruption of their own sin nature. He is overcome or conquered by his inward corruptions. This is the spiritual state of the fallen human race, and it was true of the Galatians before their conversion.

This enslavement to sin was once true of us all before coming to Christ. We, too, once lived without the knowledge of God. In that lost state, we were in bondage to sin. We knew *about* God, but we did not know Him. Even if we grew up in the church and had an exposure to the Bible, we were spiritually ignorant of God before we were converted. In an unregenerate state, we were without a saving relationship with God. We may have heard others talking *about* God. We may have heard sermons *about* God. But we were ignorant of Him. That is the state in which unbelievers exist.

This is where Paul begins this section in which he denounces their legalism. He must remind the Galatian church of their past enslavement to sin and idols. The point of his argument will be: Why have you returned to a state of slavery after being delivered from it?

Their Powerful Conversion to Christ

Paul next reminds the Galatians of their conversion to God. Verse 9 begins with two decisive words: "But now." That signals that something dramatically different has occurred in their lives. Paul writes: "But now that you have come to know God." That is the greatest change that could occur in anyone's life. They once did not know God, but now have come to know

Him. That is, they have come to know God personally and intimately through faith in Jesus Christ. Paul and Barnabas had come to the cities of Galatia to preach the gospel when they were ignorant of God (Acts 13:13–14:20). Through the power of the gospel and the work of the Holy Spirit, they were drawn to faith in Christ. In that moment, they were delivered from darkness to light. They were transferred from their ignorance of God to the personal knowledge of Him. This word "know" is the Greek word *ginokso,* which means more than merely to know about something intellectually. Rather, it means to know someone personally and experientially. It is synonymous with loving someone in a close relationship. To know God is to enter into a saving relationship with Him.

The prophet Jeremiah stated that knowing God is the greatest knowledge of all: "Let not a wise man boast of his wisdom, and let not the mighty man boast of his might. Let not a rich man boast of his riches, but let him who boasts boast of this that he understands and knows Me" (Jeremiah 9:23). Knowing God is what we should brag about. Here is our boast, namely that lowly sinners on this earth can know the living God, the One who has spoken everything into being out of nothing. When Paul says, "But now that you have come to know God," this change points back to their conversion to Christ.

In John 10:14, Jesus affirmed: "I know My own and My own know Me." This means that Christ's sheep know Him in a personal way. Their knowledge of Christ is not a secondhand knowledge, but is found in a direct relationship with Him. They are not merely distantly acquainted with Him by external religion. Instead, knowing Christ is entering into a vital, living relationship with Him. It is far more real than any other relationship one has. It is more vibrant, more dynamic, than any other human relationship one enjoys. We fellowship and commune with Him within our souls.

In John 17:3, Jesus asserted: "This is eternal life, that they may know You the only true God and Jesus Christ whom You have sent." To have eternal life is to know God intimately one's heart. Paul speaks of "the surpassing value of knowing Christ Jesus, my Lord" (Philippians 3:8). Nothing compares with knowing Him. The chief pursuit of Paul's life was "that I may know Him" (Philippians 3:10). Paul ran the race that God put before him, with every stride propelling him forward, that he might know Christ more closely, more deeply, and more personally.

In this Galatians text, Paul makes a very important theological distinction about knowing God: "Now that you have come to know God, or rather to be known by God" (verse 9). The apostle asserted that they knew God, but, more importantly, that they had come to be known by God. This emphasizes that the initiative in this relationship had been taken by God. The reason that they had come to know God is that He had made Himself known to them. In that sense, they had come to know God.

Paul knew from his own conversion experience on the Damascus road that it was God who sought to know him. At the time, Paul was going with letters in hand to apprehend the Christians and drag them back to Jerusalem that they might be put on trial to face death. Full of religious zeal, he was going to persecute the believers and tear down the church. In that moment, though, Christ sovereignly appeared to Paul. Paul was not even seeking Him, yet Christ dramatically intervened, literally knocking him off his high horse. All that Paul could do was look up into the blazing light that was brighter than the noonday sun. In that instant, Paul was converted to Christ. He cried out, "Who are You, Lord" (Acts 9:5)?

It was sovereign grace that converted him, conquering his proud heart. Christ appeared and did not merely knock on the door to his heart. Jesus knocked the door down. Jesus came declaring, "You are known by God. You are Mine." As a result, Paul suddenly came to know the Lord Jesus Christ, and to know God. Paul had been previously known by God, or foreknown by Him. That is, he was personally loved by God in a saving relationship. This saving was by God's initiative, not by Paul's seeking. God was active, Paul was passive.

Concerning the Galatians' conversion, John Calvin, the Genevan Reformer, comments: "God had visited them in His mercy." That the Galatians knew God was certainly not the result of their own search. The Bible says: "There is none who seeks for God" (Romans 3:11; cf. Psalm 14:2–3; 53:2–3). It was by the sovereign operation of God that He made Himself known to them in an irresistible, saving way.

The difference in the voice of the verbs used by the apostle here must be carefully noted. Paul intentionally changes from the active voice in the first verb, "you have come to know God," to the passive voice in the second verb where he says, "or rather to be known by God." The reason that they knew God was that God chose to make Himself known to them. The stress here is on the divine initiative, which is traced back to the doctrines of sovereign election and effectual grace. The words "to be known by God" imply that it was the result of the divine choice and calling. By unconditional election, Paul was chosen and predetermined to be known by God. This saving knowledge by God is rooted and grounded in the eternal counsels of Almighty God, established before the world began. That is what "foreknowledge" means, namely to be sovereignly chosen by God for salvation in eternity past.

There are many verses in the Old and the New Testaments that speak to what it means to be known by God. In Psalm 1:6, the psalmist writes: "For the Lord knows the way of the righteous, but the way of the wicked will perish." God is saying that He has far more than a mere awareness of the way of the righteous. The reference is to the personal intimacy and close involvement that He has with His own. By contrast, God does not know the way of the wicked. Though He knows everything *about* the path the unrighteous take, He is far removed from them. He has no personal relationship with the wicked. On the last day, God's infallible record of every unbeliever's life will be brought forth because He knows everything *about* them. Nevertheless, God does not know them. But to the contrary, God knows the way of the righteous.

In Amos 3:2, God addresses the nation Israel through the prophet: "You only I have chosen among all the families of the earth." The word "chosen" is actually the Hebrew word "known (yādah)." Among all the families of the earth, God says, He only knows the families of His chosen nation, Israel. God has selectively decreed to know His elect people.

In Nahum 1:7, the Bible states: "The Lord is good, a stronghold in a day of trouble; and He knows those who take refuge in Him." Here, God knows those who have entrusted their lives to Him. To be known by God means to be in a saving relationship with Him. Yet, in Matthew 7:23, Jesus warns: "And then I will declare to them, 'I never knew you.' " Though God knows everything about everyone, He does not know the wicked. This passage is not speaking of His cognitive knowledge of facts about people, but His saving knowledge of those who are genuinely converted. Jesus said there are many who claim to know Him, but He does not know them. In the Parable of the Ten Virgins, five were foolish and the other five were wise. To the foolish, Jesus said: "Later the other virgins also came, saying, 'Lord, lord, open up for us.' But He answered, 'Truly I say to you, I do not know you' " (Matthew 25:11–12). That is to say, they were never known by Christ.

In John 10:14, Jesus said: "I am the Good Shepherd; and I know My own, and My own know Me." This word speaks of the intimate, personal relationship that exists between the Savior and sinners, who turn to Him in genuine repentance and saving faith. Jesus savingly knows them. In John 10:27, Jesus stated" "My sheep hear My voice and I know them." Simply put, Christ knows His own sheep.

This saving relationship with God began in eternity past when the Father chose His elect. In distinguishing love, God set His heart upon them before He created the world. In Romans 8:29, Paul identifies these elect ones as "those whom He foreknew." This text does not say, "For *what* He *foresaw*," as if God was looking down the tunnel of time to learn what He did not previously know. It does not say, "*What* He foresaw," as though He was seeing events and circumstances involving the conversion of sinners. God has never looked ahead and learned anything. Rather, this reads "*whom*," a personal pronoun. God foreknew individuals; He did not foresee events. It was "whom He foreknew," that "He also predestined to become conformed to the image of His Son." Foreknowledge means to be previously loved by God in a saving way. Romans 9:13 makes this clear: "Jacob I loved, but Esau I hated." The saving love of God is reserved for His elect only.

"Foreknowledge" refers to God's predetermined choice to set His love upon certain individuals. It is God's sovereign choice to love His elect. It was not an arbitrary choice, but one made with eternal love. Romans 11:2 states: "God has not rejected His people whom He foreknew." Once God has foreknown His own in eternity past, that one will never be rejected by Him within time. In 1 Corinthians 8:3, Paul writes: "If anyone loves God, he is known by Him." This says, if anyone loves God it is because they were first known by Him. 2 Timothy 2:19 maintains that "the firm foundation of Lord stands, having this seal, 'The Lord knows those who are His.' " The Lord knows *about* the entire world, but He only knows His elect. That is to say, the Lord knows His own people, the few who are on the narrow path.

In 1 Peter 1:1–2, Peter asserts that believers were "chosen according to the foreknowledge of God." Here, foreknowledge speaks to a predetermined relationship that God initiated with some before they were born. God has been so intentional in the exercise of His love that He has foreknown His elect from before the foundation of the world. His heart is so strong toward His elect that many waters cannot quench the flame of His eternal love towards them. This immutable, eternal love of God has resulted in the salvation of His chosen ones. John MacArthur explains this verse this way: "We can know God only because He first knew us, just as we chose Him only because He first chose us. We love Him only because He first loved us." This basic principle of theology teaches that God is always the First Cause in salvation, and man is the responder.

S. Lewis Johnson tells the story of a little boy who was asked by a very zealous Christian witness, "Little boy, have you found Jesus?" To which the little boy replied, "Why, no, sir, I did not know Jesus was lost. But I was lost, and He found me." That is the way salvation works. It is God knowing us long before we knew Him.

This is what Paul is saying to the Galatians. They know God only because they have come to be known by Him. Every one who was known by God ought to be deeply humbled and ask, "Why me, God? Out of this vast universe, out of this entire human race, why would You choose to know me? Why would the King of the universe choose to love me?"

Have you asked yourself lately why God would choose to know you? If you are in Christ, you can be assured that the King of heaven chose to love you in a saving way from all eternity past. He selected you out of all humanity, to know you intimately and personally. Because He first loved you, you have come to enjoy a personal relationship with the living God.

This truth is important in combating legalism. There is nothing that we can do to commend ourselves toward God. It was by sovereign grace that God chose to love us, long before we ever believed in Christ. God did not love us because of anything attractive in our lives. God chose us not because of us, but in spite of us. Therefore, all our efforts to keep man-made rules to gain acceptance with Him should be forsaken.

Their Present Drift Towards Legalism

Paul's instruction for the Galatians' finally leads him to address their present drift towards legalism. Paul writes these sad words: "How is it that you turn back again to the weak and worthless elemental things, to which you desire to be enslaved all over again" (verse 9)? There is a sense of astonishment and amazement by Paul as he records this. It is as if he were saying, "Can you explain something to me? How is it that you have turned back again toward legalism after being saved by divine, sovereign grace? How is it that you have done a complete reversal? How is it that you have done an about-face in your spiritual life?" The phrase "turned back again" is in the present tense. This means, they were in the ongoing, continual process of turning back to "the weak and worthless elemental things."

Paul described their legalism this way: "You turn back again to the weak and worthless elemental things" (verse 9). That is, that to which they had returned, specifically their legalism, was not profound nor powerful, but weak, worthless, and elementary. It is "weak," having no power to sanctify or satisfy them. In their overcoming sin, their legalism was absolutely impotent. Further, their strict rules were "worthless," devoid of any ability to affect real spiritual growth in their lives. Moreover their legalism consisted of "elemental things," that which is juvenile, childish, and immature. Legalism was turning them away from their relationship with the living God, who had made Himself known to them. They had turned away from the truth for a false standard of spiritual living.

Previously, they had been ensnared by their sin and set free by the Lord Jesus Christ. "If the Son shall set you free, you shall be free indeed" (John 8:36). But now, having been set free by the Lord Jesus Christ, they have been brought back into spiritual bondage again. They have come under the influence of the Judaizers, the false teachers who were luring them back under the ceremonial law in the Old Testament that has already been fulfilled in the cross of the Lord Jesus Christ. Paul calls this legalism "weak and worthless," merely "elemental things" that brings absolutely no ability to mature and grow believers.

Instead, this kind of legalism is a hindrance, causing him to assert: "You desire to be enslaved all over again." By these words, Paul is maintaining, "You have exchanged one prison cell for another." In other words, "Christ has set you free from your enslavement to your flesh and the world. Having liberated you to walk in triumph over your old life in sin, you have turned back and checked yourself into a different prison cell and locked the door. You have slammed yourself into the dark cell of legalism that profits your spiritual life nothing."

Paul proceeds to give specific examples of legalism: "You observe days and months and seasons and years" (verse 10). "Days" refers to sabbatical days that were required under the old covenant in Israel before the coming of Christ. These sabbatical days were a picture of the rest a believer has in the Lord. These days of rest symbolize the spiritual rest of the one who trusts Christ for salvation. He has ceased striving to work his way to heaven. This Sabbath rest foreshadowed the perfect rest believers have in Jesus Christ. When Christ came into this world through His death upon the cross, He fulfilled every ceremonial law and type and prophecy. The veil was wrent top to bottom in the Temple, signifying that the Old Testament, Judaistic, ceremonial system was ancient history. It was nothing more than shadow, the substance being Christ Himself. The reality of Christ has now come.

Paul's reasoning is: "Now that you have come to faith in Christ, why would you turn away from Him and go back to mere shadows?" That is what legalism is. Why would they go back to keep these sabbatical day festivals when they have the reality of Christ? Under the new covenant, these Sabbath days had no spiritual value whatsoever. They were merely a sign and a picture of the coming reality of Jesus Christ at the cross.

As Paul confronts them, "months" refers to new moon celebrations. "Seasons" are the great feasts, such as the Passover Feast and the Feast of Tabernacles. "Years" refers to Jubilee years and sabbatical years. These false teachers were actually trying to bring believers back under the Old Covenant. All of these were fulfilled in the death of Christ for sinners. At the cross, the entire sacrificial system was abolished, as well as the ceremonial laws. But these Galatian believers were allowing themselves to be put back under the Old Covenant. Paul says that they were "being enslaved all over again."

As ministers of the New Covenant, we are not slitting the throat of a lamb or of a goat in church and placing the sacrifice on the altar. We are not walking down the aisle with a sensor and waving it back and forth, proceeding out of the courtyard of the Gentiles into the holy place. We are not going behind a screen or veil into the supposed Holy of Holies. Such things are weak and worthless.

With a pastor's broken heart, Paul laments: "I fear for you" (verse 11). Paul does not commend their dabbling in legalism. Rather he says, "I fear for you" because their souls were in great spiritual danger. Paul knew that they were being held back in their maturity. They were being severely restricted from growing in the grace and knowledge of the Lord Jesus Christ. Legalism was a major hindrance to their spiritual development that was pulling them away from Christ.

Paul bemoans: "I have labored over you in vain." If they remained in the snare of legalism, he feared that his pastoral efforts had been futile. Paul had suffered greatly for the Galatians on his first missionary journey that he might bring the gospel to them. Paul was stoned to the point of death in Lystra, drug outside the city, and left for dead. Paul plunged ahead into city after city, going into synagogues, preaching the gospel of Christ, absorbing the opposition and persecution. The Apostle Paul labored over them, paying a high price to bring them the gospel truth. In so many words, he is saying, "I fear that perhaps I have labored over you in vain, that my ministry towards you has proven to be null and void. All my sacrifice on your behalf apparently did not amount to anything. You obviously did not hear what I said. The truth must not have registered with you. It obviously did not connect with you, because look at you. You are not living by the standard of the Word of

God. You have gone back to false things that are enslaving and ensnaring you."

The Galatians desperately needed to resist every form of legalism, and so must we. Wherever we see legalism, we need to resist its every encroachment. We need to reject it because it will hold back believers from growing into spiritual maturity. Legalism turns away a congregation from the living Christ in order to embrace that which has no spiritual value to aid their spiritual development. Rather, every believer must look to Christ and follow Him, looking to the Word and trusting in the Spirit. Let all who name the name of Christ be riveted upon Him. Let us thank God that we have come to be known by Him. Let us rejoice that once and for all time Christ has fulfilled the entirety of the Old Testament ceremonial law.

Let us rejoice that the truth of the gospel has set us free from sin and death. Let us thank God that the Lord Jesus Christ has made Himself known to us by His Word. We have come as those who know God, or, rather, to be known by Him. May we avoid the danger of legalism at all costs. And may God, by His Word and Spirit, mature us into true Christlikeness.

Obedience:
Love or Legalism?

John MacArthur

A few years ago I wrote a book that became the subject of widespread controversy. That book, *The Gospel According to Jesus*, argued that Jesus is presented in the gospel as both Savior *and* Lord, and He demands obedience. To be precise, Jesus is actually *never* presented as "Savior and Lord" in the Bible; it is *always* as "Lord and Savior." Therefore, those who remain obstinately unwilling to obey Him are actually guilty of rejecting the Christ who is offered in the gospel. So the person who claims to accept Jesus as Savior while persisting to refuse His lordship has actually spurned the true Christ and therefore is no Christian.

That, of course, is nothing more or less than what mainstream evangelicalism has historically affirmed. Virtually all the important Protestant statements of faith say exactly the same thing. In the Westminster Shorter Catechism, for example, Question 86 asks, "What is faith in Jesus Christ?" The answer: "Faith in Jesus Christ is a saving grace, whereby we receive and rest upon Him alone for salvation, *as He is offered to us in the gospel*" (emphasis added). Question 87 goes on to define repentance unto life as "a saving grace, whereby a sinner, out of a true sense of his sin, and apprehension of the mercy of God in Christ, doth, with grief and hatred of his sin, turn from it unto God, *with full purpose of, and endeavor after, new obedience*" (emphasis added).

Our obedience does not *merit* salvation, of course. But genuine conversion to Christ inevitably produces obedience. Therefore, while obedience is never a *condition* for salvation, it is nonetheless always salvation's *fruit*. That is why Scripture speaks of

obedience as an essential evidence of true Christianity: "He that
saith, I know Him, and keepeth not His commandments, is a
liar, and the truth is not in him" (1 John 2:4). "In this the children of God are manifest, and the children of the devil: whosoever doeth not righteousness is not of God" (3:10). "He that
doeth good is of God: but he that doeth evil hath not seen God"
(3 John 11).

Do We Obey Out of Love or Out of Duty?
     In the midst of the controversy over these things, a fellow
pastor wrote me:

> Dear John,
>   I am sympathetic to your stance on the lord-
> ship of Christ. You are quite right in teaching that
> the gospel calls sinners to repentance and calls for
> their obedience to Christ as Lord. His lordship is
> as crucial to the gospel message as His deity. In
> fact, as you point out, His deity and His lordship
> are so inextricably bound together that a Christ
> who is not Lord of all is not the Christ who saves.
> The modern notion that the sinner can reject
> Christ as Lord but receive Him as Savior is foreign
> to all the historic creeds. To my way of thinking,
> any message that excludes the lordship of Christ is
> not the gospel at all.
>   If you don't mind, however, I would like to of-
> fer a criticism that I hope you will find helpful, not
> hurtful: I notice that you present Christian obedi-
> ence as a *duty*. You often cite the biblical passages
> that speak of the Christian as a bondservant, as if
> this meant we are abject slaves to Him. Your stress
> is on the Lord's authority to command obedience.
> And therefore you speak of obedience as an *obliga-
> tion* to which the believer is bound.
>   I see a different emphasis in Scripture. Faith
> works through love (Galatians 5:6). The Christian
> obeys Christ out of sheer love for Him. Obedience

for the Christian is not so much a duty as it is a delight. Believers obey because that is where they
find their satisfaction, *not* because they are bound
to do so. We obey out of love for Christ, not out of
fear, and not out of duty. I believe this perspective
is essential to joyous Christian living. It is the
whole difference between legalism and true Christianity.

I sincerely appreciated that man's comments. And I agree
that it is possible to place so much stress on the *duty* of obedience that we lose sight of the *joy* of it. After all, the Christian's
obedience should be a delight. Love for Christ is a higher motive
than fear. So there is certainly some sound truth in what this
man wrote.

Nonetheless, the danger of overemphasis is very real on both
sides of this truth. It is not quite right to say "We obey out of
love for Christ . . . and *not* out of duty." Duty and love are not
incompatible motives. A father provides for his children because
he loves them. Yet it is also his legal and moral duty to do so.
The fact that a man loves his children does not lessen his duty to
them. The more he loves them, the more he will see the duty as
a joy and not a drudgery. But even when the duty is a delight, it
should not diminish the father's solemn sense of duty.

Our obedience to Christ is like that. Certainly we ought to
obey Him out of a deep love for Him. And the sheer joy of
pleasing Him should permeate our obedience. Yet we should
never think of obedience as anything less than a sacred duty.
Our love for Christ does not make submission to Him elective.
Christ is still our Master, and our relationship with Him carries a
great weight of responsibility. We ought to serve Him as loving,
devoted bondservants. "Abject slaves" is probably not too strong
a term.

Jesus Himself underscored this very thing:

But which of you, having a servant plowing or

feeding cattle, will say unto him by and by, when
he is come from the field, Go and sit down to
meat? And will not rather say unto him, Make
ready wherewith I may sup, and gird thyself, and
serve me, till I have eaten and drunken; and after-
ward thou shalt eat and drink? Doth he thank that
servant because he did the things that were commanded him? I trow not. So likewise ye, when ye
shall have done all those things which are commanded you, say, We are unprofitable servants; we
have done that which was our duty to do (Luke
17:7–10).

That imagery paints a clear picture of the kind of servitude
we are expected to render to Christ as His servants.

But that's only half the picture. Our Lord also called for the
obedience of love: "If ye love Me, keep My commandments"
(John 14:15). And He elevated those who obey to the level of
friends:

Ye are My friends, if ye do whatsoever I command
you. Henceforth I call you not servants; for the servant knoweth not what his lord doeth: but I have
called you friends; for all things that I have heard
of My Father I have made known unto you (John
15:14–15).

Obviously, our Lord viewed our love for Him and our duty
to Him as motives for obedience that are inextricably and necessarily bound together: "He that hath My commandments, and
keepeth them, he it is that loveth Me" (John 14:21). "If ye keep
My commandments, ye shall abide in My love; even as I have
kept My Father's commandments, and abide in His love" (John
15:10).

Far from being a drudgery, Christian obedience is thus the
bond of our relationship with Christ and the source of our deep-
est joy. And the fact that we are obliged to submit to His lord-

ship should never alter the joy we find in doing so.

Of course, because we are still fleshly creatures, our obedience is not *always* joyful. And so we must realize that even when our hearts are not brimming with the joy of the Lord, obedience remains our duty. We are to obey when it brings us pleasure, but we also must obey even when we do not feel like it. *Both* our love for the Lord and our sense of duty to Him should motivate this obedience. One must never cancel out the other.

I fear that the church in our generation is losing sight of the role of duty in the Christian life. Multitudes see "duty" as something altogether foreign to Christianity. Compliance with the commandments of Christ is deemed optional. If you dare suggest that obedience is mandatory, you will be branded a legalist.

"We are not under the law, but under grace" has become the mantra of modern Christianity. But most who chant that phrase today mean something dramatically different from what the apostle Paul meant in Romans 6:14 when he wrote, "Ye are not under the law, but under grace."

In What Sense Are We Freed from the Law Under Grace?

The phrase "under the law" occurs at least ten times in Paul's epistles, so we know it is a crucial concept in his theology. In Galatians 3:23, for example, He writes, "Before faith came, we were kept *under the law*." Now, however, he says as Christians we are "*not* under the law" (Galatians 5:18).

I often hear Christians recite the phrase "not under the law, but under grace" as if it meant no standard of law whatsoever is ever binding on believers. Grace is seen as a grand permissiveness, contrasting with the uncompromising moral standard of the law. One man wrote:

> According to Paul, I am not under law. That has radical practical consequences for my Christian life. It means I do not have to look over my shoulder at the law and judge my life by it. The law was a negative standard. It was filled with prohibitions

and punishments. Grace is the opposite. It is filled with positive inducements and promises. Which would you rather have as a rule of life? *I live under grace, not law.* And that means whenever the law brings its negative message—*when it says, "thou shalt not"*—it does not apply to me.

The notion that no law is binding on the Christian is a classic form of *antinomianism.* This type of thinking sets grace *against* law, as if the two were antithetical. It has some dire theological consequences.

It is crucial to understand that in terms of moral standards, grace does not permit what the law prohibits. Grace never signifies the lowering of God's moral demands. The word "grace" in Scripture signifies a lot of things, but licentiousness is not one of them. In fact, those who turn the grace of God into promiscuity are expressly condemned as false teachers (Jude 4).

Grace, according to Scripture, is the undeserved kindness of a sovereign God. More than that, grace means that God mercifully gives us the very opposite of what our sin merits. Grace includes not merely pardon for our sin, but also the power to live a transformed life. In other words, the grace Scripture describes is a dynamic force, the sovereign influence of a holy God operating in the lives of undeserving sinners. This is the key to grace: it is God working in us to secure our working for Him (Philippians 2:13). Grace first transforms the heart and thus makes the believer wholly willing to trust and obey. Grace then conveys upon us both the desire and the strength to fulfill God's good pleasure. Far more than mere pardon, grace also insures our obedience, gives us a true love for God, and transforms our lives in every sense.

Ultimately, grace totally conforms us to the image of Christ (Romans 8:29). Even now, grace is doing what the law could not do: it is fulfilling the righteous requirement of the law in us (Romans 8:3–4).

So the moral standard set by the law does not change under

grace. Indeed, it could not; it is a reflection of God's character. But divine grace actually empowers us to fulfill the moral demands of the law in a way that the law alone could never do.

Just what *does* the apostle Paul mean when he says we are not under law? There are two ways in which Scripture clearly teaches we are not under law:

1. *We are not under the ceremonial law.*

Paul's epistle to the Galatians uses the expression "under the law" several times (3:23; 4:4–5, 21; 5:18). Paul wrote this epistle to confront the influence of the Judaizers, Jewish legalists who were trying to impose the ceremonies and rituals of the Mosaic law on all Christians. According to the Judaizers, in order to become a true Christian, a Gentile first had to become a Jewish proselyte.

Circumcision and the dietary laws became the test issues. This had been a running dispute in the early church from the very beginning. The earliest church council in Jerusalem had been convened to deal with this very question. According to Acts 15:5, some Pharisees who had converted to Christianity rose up and demanded that Gentiles who joined the church be circumcised and directed to obey the law of Moses. Luke records what happened:

> And the apostles and elders came together for to consider of this matter. And when there had been much disputing, Peter rose up, and said unto them, Men and brethren, ye know how that a good while ago God made choice among us, that the Gentiles by my mouth should hear the word of the gospel, and believe. And God, which knoweth the hearts, bare them witness, giving them the Holy Ghost, even as He did unto us; and put no difference between us and them, purifying their hearts by faith. Now therefore why tempt ye God, to put a yoke upon the neck of the disciples, which neither our fathers nor we were able to bear? But we believe that through the grace of the Lord Jesus

Christ we shall be saved, even as they (Acts 15:6–
11).

The council saw a heated debate on the question. But, led by
James, they ultimately came to consensus:

Trouble not them, which from among the Gentiles
are turned to God: but . . . write unto them, that
they abstain from pollutions of idols, and from fornication, and from things strangled, and from
blood (verses 19–20).

This meant that the ceremonial requirements of the Mosaic
law were not to be imposed upon the church. Circumcision
could not be required of the Gentiles. Strict adherence to the
dietary laws was not to be prescribed. But in order not to offend
the Jewish brethren, the Gentiles were asked to abstain from the
most offensive dietary practices: the eating of meat offered to
idols, of strangled animals, and of blood. Even those restrictions
were not imposed as binding matters of legal necessity, but were
required of the Gentiles only as a matter of charity toward their
Jewish brethren.

How do we know that these prohibitions against eating certain things were not meant to be a permanent standard for the
church for all time? As Paul wrote to Timothy, nothing is to be
viewed as ceremonially unclean if it is received with thanksgiving (1 Timothy 4:4). But these measures were called for by the
Jerusalem Council in the primitive church as a matter of charity
to the many Jewish believers who saw such practices as inherently pagan. The Apostle Paul summed up this principle of freedom and deference in Romans 14:14–15:

I know, and am persuaded by the Lord Jesus, that
there is nothing unclean of itself: but to him that
esteemeth any thing to be unclean, to him it is unclean. But if thy brother be grieved with thy meat,

now walkest thou not charitably.

A side note is necessary here with regard to the restriction against "fornication." The biblical prohibitions against fornication are moral, not ceremonial, commandments. So why was it necessary to include a ban on fornication in the Jerusalem Council's instructions? After all, fornication would clearly be deemed morally reprehensible and strictly forbidden under *any* standard in the early church. And from the beginning the dispute that prompted the Jerusalem Council had to do only with the ceremonial aspects of Moses' law.

The answer lies in an understanding of the pagan religions from which many of these Gentile converts had come. The practice of ceremonial fornication was common. Many of the pagan shrines featured temple prostitutes, with whom acts of fornication were deemed religious experiences. So when it forbade "pollutions of idols, and . . . fornication," the Council was prohibiting the observance of pagan religious ceremonies. And when it called for abstinence "from things strangled, and from blood," it was asking the Gentiles to have respect for the deeply ingrained scruples of their Jewish brethren, which resulted from lifelong obedience to Mosaic ceremonies.

In other words, pagan religious ceremonies were forbidden, and Jewish ceremonies were not made the standard. But charity was enjoined upon all.

It is crucial to see that this Council was explicitly *not* establishing the Mosaic ceremonial law *or any portion of it* as the standard for the church. The New Testament is explicit throughout that the types and ceremonies of the Law are *not* binding on Christians. The dietary and ceremonial requirements of Moses' law "are a shadow of things to come; but the body is of Christ" (Colossians 2:17). The priesthood and temple worship of the Old Testament economy also "serve unto the example and shadow of heavenly things" (Hebrews 8:5). Christ is the fulfillment of all those observances, and He is the Mediator of a new covenant. To cling to the types and shadows of the old covenant is in effect to deny that Christ, the One foreshadowed, is superior. Therefore, the ceremonial aspects of Moses' law have no place whatsoever in the Church.

Why did both Paul and the writer of Hebrews view the Judaizers' doctrine as such a serious error? Because by retreating to the types and shadows of the old covenant, these people were guilty of replacing the all-important reality of a living Savior with outmoded symbols that only *pointed* to Him. Their attachment to those now-barren religious emblems *necessarily* thrust them into a system of works. To return to the old covenant was a *de facto* rejection of Christ in favor of obsolete types and symbols.

In one of the most unusual encounters between two apostles recorded anywhere in Scripture, Peter and Paul had a very public conflict over the question of obedience to the ceremonial law. Paul describes the confrontation in Galatians 2:11–14:

> When Peter was come to Antioch, I withstood him to the face, because he was to be blamed. For before that certain came from James, he did eat with the Gentiles: but when they were come, he withdrew and separated himself, fearing them which were of the circumcision. And the other Jews dissembled likewise with him; insomuch that Barnabas also was carried away with their dissimulation. But when I saw that they walked not uprightly according to the truth of the gospel, I said unto Peter before them all, If thou, being a Jew, livest after the manner of Gentiles, and not as do the Jews, why compellest thou the Gentiles to live as do the Jews?

The issue at stake here was no longer the question of charity toward Jewish brethren, but the whole doctrine of justification by faith. Apparently, even after the Jerusalem Council had rendered its decision, the Judaizers nevertheless reverted to demanding circumcision for every Gentile convert. They were actually suggesting that observance of the ceremonial law was essential for justification. And, as Paul suggests, Peter, of all people, should have known better: "Knowing that a man is not justified by the works of the law, but by the faith of Jesus Christ, even we have believed in Jesus Christ, that we might be justified by the faith of Christ, and not by the works of the law: for by the works of the law shall no flesh be justified" (verse 16).

2. *We are not under the law for justification.*

The centerpiece of New Testament theology is justification by faith. This is the doctrine that makes Christianity distinct. Every other religion in the world teaches some system of human merit. Christianity alone teaches that the merit necessary for our salvation is supplied by God on our behalf.

Justification is defined theologically as that act of God whereby He declares the believing sinner righteous. When God justifies a sinner, he looks at the person and says, "I accept that person as completely righteous." It is a divine "not guilty" verdict, and more. It elevates the sinner from the condemnation he deserves to a position of divine privilege in Christ.

Justification poses a huge theological problem. Proverbs 17:15 says, "He that justifieth the wicked, and he that condemneth the just, even they both are abomination to the Lord." In other words, God Himself strictly forbids us to declare a guilty person righteous. And God says definitively in Exodus 23:7, "I will not justify the wicked."

Two obstacles exist with regard to justifying sinners. One is our sin. We accumulate guilt every time we sin, and true justice demands that every sin be punished. To let an evildoer go unpunished is by definition unjust. So God is obligated by His own perfect standard of justice to exact a full penalty for every sin.

The second obstacle to justification is our utter lack of merit. Not only do we accumulate guilt (or demerit) every time we sin, but we also lack the necessary merit. Even if our slate could be completely wiped clean, all we would have would be a blank slate. But in order to be acceptable to God, we are required to have the full merit that comes with perfect obedience to His law. Forgiveness for our sin isn't enough. We still need the merit of an absolutely perfect righteousness (Matthew 5:20, 48).

From the human perspective, those would seem to be impossible obstacles to the justification of any sinner. We can certainly understand the disciples' bewilderment when they saw these same difficulties: "Who then can be saved?" (Matthew 19:25).

However, there were people in Paul's day who thought that if they could just be as good as they could possibly be, they might earn enough merit to please God. This was the attitude behind the Judaizers' insistence on adhering to the ceremonial laws. They were trying to justify themselves before God through their own works.

They were trying to earn their own righteousness. That is the very definition of "self-righteous." Jesus' Sermon on the Mount was an attack on that kind of thinking. He pointed to the Pharisees, legalists who kept the law more fastidiously than anyone else. By human standards they were as "good" as it is possible to be. But Jesus said their goodness is simply not good enough to earn God's favor: "I say unto you that except your righteousness shall exceed the righteousness of the scribes and Pharisees, ye shall in no case enter into the kingdom of heaven" (Matthew 5:20).

Jesus was teaching as plainly as possible that God will be pleased with nothing but an absolutely perfect righteousness. He taught that it is not good enough to avoid killing; we must also avoid the sin of hatred (verse 22). He said if you lust in your heart, it is the same as committing adultery (verse 28). He set the standard as high as possible, and then said that if you don't attain that perfect standard of righteousness, you cannot enter the kingdom of heaven. And thus He condemned us all.

The Apostle James destroyed any vestige of hope we might have of being justified by law when he wrote, "Whosoever shall keep the whole law, and yet offend in one point, he is guilty of all" (James 2:10).

What are we supposed to conclude? That we cannot be justified by the works of the law. It is utterly impossible. The apostle

Paul underscores this same truth again and again:

> Ye could not be justified by the law of Moses (Acts
> 13:39).

> What things soever the law saith, it saith to them
> who are under the law: that every mouth may be
> stopped, and all the world may become guilty be-
> fore God. Therefore by the deeds of the law there
> shall no flesh be justified in his sight: for by the
> law is the knowledge of sin" (Romans 3:19–20).

> The law worketh wrath (Romans 4:15).

> As many as are of the works of the law are under
> the curse: for it is written, Cursed is every one that
> continueth not in all things which are written in
> the book of the law to do them . . . No man is jus-
> tified by the law in the sight of God (Galatians
> 3:10–11).

Paul could not state it any more clearly than that. To make
the fatal mistake of thinking you can be justified by being good
enough to make yourself acceptable to God is to put yourself
under the condemnation of the law.

This was the heart of the problem in Galatia. People were
teaching that it was necessary to obey the law *in order to be justified.* In chapter 1 Paul calls this "another gospel," and he pronounces a solemn curse on those who were teaching it.

When Paul spoke of those who were "under the law," he was
speaking of people who thought they could be justified by obedience to the law. Two parallel expressions in Galatians make
this extremely clear. One is Galatians 4:21: "Tell me, *ye that desire to be under the law,* do ye not hear the law?" (emphasis
added). If they had listened to the law itself, they would have
heard that it establishes impossible conditions for justification. It
condemns those who fail to obey it. For sinners, the law could be

a means of condemnation, but *never* a means of justification.

For a sinner to embrace the law as a means of justification is sheer folly. Yet there were those in Galatia who "desire[d] to be under the law" (4:21).

Notice the parallel expression in Galatians 5:4: "You who are seeking to be justified by law" (New American Standard Bible). Those who were seeking to be "justified by law" in Galatians 5:4 were the same as those who desired to be "under the law" in 4:21.

Therefore, to be "under the law" in Paul's terminology is to be *under the law as a means of justification.* It is crucial to understand how Paul uses this expression. When he says we are not under the law but under grace in Romans 6, he is not discarding the *moral teachings* of the law. He is not lending credence to any sort of antinomian doctrine. He is not minimizing the sin of disobedience to the moral teachings of the law. He is not disparaging the law itself. In fact, in Romans 7:12, he calls the law "holy, just, and good."

Paul's consistent teaching with regard to the law is that it can never be a means of justification. And when he says we are "not under law," he means we do not ground our justification in our own personal obedience.

We are no longer trying to justify ourselves by obedience to the law. We are justified by grace through faith, not by the works of the law (Galatians 2:16). And therefore we are no longer under the condemnation of the law.

How Can God Justify the Ungodly?

How, then, can we be justified? How can God declare guilty sinners righteous without lowering or compromising His own righteous standard?

The answer lies in the work of Christ on our behalf. In Galatians 4:4, the apostle states that Jesus Christ was born "under the law." Obviously, this does not mean merely that Jesus was born Jewish. It means that He was *under the law* in the Pauline sense, obligated to fulfill the law perfectly as a means of justification.

In this same context, in the span of two verses, Paul twice employs the phrase "under the law." There is a clear logical connection between the last phrase in verse 4 and the first phrase in verse 5: Christ was "made under the law, to redeem them that were under the law."

We've already said that the law cannot be a means of righteousness for sinners. But Christ was no sinner. He lived impeccably "under the law." Hebrews 4:15 tells us He "was in all points tempted like as we are, yet without sin." He fulfilled the law perfectly, to the letter. First Peter 2:22 says He "did no sin, neither was guile found in His mouth." Hebrews 7:26 says He is "holy, harmless, undefiled, separate from sinners, and made higher than the heavens." Thus His flawless obedience to the law earned the perfect merit that is necessary to please God.

If Christ was perfectly sinless, then He did not deserve to die. As one "under the law," He would have been subject to the curse of the law if He had violated even one command, but of course He did not—He *could* not, because He is God. He fulfilled every aspect of the law to the letter—to the jot and tittle.

Yet He did die. More than that, He suffered the full wrath of God on the cross. Why? Scripture tells us the guilt of our sin was imputed to Him, and Christ paid the price for it. Consequently, the merit of His perfect obedience can be imputed to our account. That is the meaning of 2 Corinthians 5:21: God "hath made [Christ] to be sin for us, who knew no sin; that we might be made the righteousness of God in him."

His death takes care of our *guilt*, and His perfect life supplies us with all the *merit* we need to be acceptable to God. That is how God overcame the two great obstacles to our justification. And as Paul says in Romans 3:26, that is how God can remain just, and justify those who believe in Jesus. Christ has personally paid the penalty for their sin, and He has personally obtained a perfect righteousness on their behalf. So He can justify the ungodly (Romans 4:5).

Scripture teaches no other means of justification. This is at the core of all gospel truth. As early as Genesis 15:6, Scripture teaches that Abraham was justified by an imputed righteousness. Any time *any* sinner is redeemed in Scripture, it is by an imputed righteousness, not a righteousness that is somehow earned or achieved by the sinner for his own redemption.

Romans 4:6–7 says David also knew the blessedness of the man to whom God imputes righteousness apart from works. In fact, this is the whole point Paul is making in Romans 4: justification has always been by faith, not by works, and through a righteousness that is imputed to the believer. Abraham understood the doctrine of justification in that way. David knew the same truth. So from the beginning of Scripture to the end, we are taught that the only merit God accepts is a merit that is imputed to our account. He never pronounces us righteous because of our own works of righteousness.

On the contrary, God says all our righteousnesses are fatally flawed. They are of no more value to God than filthy rags (Isaiah 64:6). But that is how God sees our works—no matter how good they are by human standards. They are unacceptable, filthy, to God.

That is why *our* obedience can never be good enough. That is why those who hang their hope of heaven on their own good works only doom themselves.

How Deadly Is Legalism?

This should make it very clear that the legalism Paul condemned as "another gospel" is a brand of legalism that seeks to ground our justification in personal obedience rather than the imputed righteousness of Christ. How deadly is such legalism?

The Apostle Paul suggested it was precisely what caused the majority of Israel to reject Christ: "They being ignorant of God's righteousness, and going about to establish their own righteousness, have not submitted themselves unto the righteousness of God" (Romans 10:3).

Turning aside from the perfect righteousness of Christ (which would have been imputed to them by faith), they opted instead for an imperfect righteousness of their own. They mistakenly assumed, like most people today, that the best they could do would be good enough for God.

Here is the good news of the gospel: for everyone who believes, Christ's blood counts as payment for all our sins, and His fulfillment of the law counts as all the merit we need. Romans 10:4 therefore says, "Christ is the end [Greek, *telos*, "the thing aimed at"] of the law for righteousness to every one that believeth." Christ is the fulfillment of everything the law intended. In Christ, the ultimate goal of the law, *a perfect righteousness,* is made available to every believer. His righteousness is imputed to us by faith, and that is why God accepts us in Christ and for Christ's sake.

To the Apostle Paul himself, this truth had deeply personal implications. He had labored his whole life as a legalistic Pharisee trying to establish his own righteousness by the law. He described his efforts in Philippians 3:4–8:

> If any other man thinketh that he hath whereof he might trust in the flesh, I more: circumcised the eighth day, of the stock of Israel, of the tribe of Benjamin, a Hebrew of the Hebrews; as touching the law, a Pharisee; concerning zeal, persecuting the church; touching the righteousness which is in the law, blameless. But what things were gain to me, those I counted loss for Christ. Yea doubtless, and I count all things but loss for the excellency of the knowledge of Christ Jesus my Lord: for whom I have suffered the loss of all things, and do count them but dung, that I may win Christ.

What was so important to Paul about dumping all his own righteousness? Why did he count a whole lifetime of good works as mere rubbish? Because he knew it was flawed. And he knew that in Christ he would be the recipient of a perfect righteousness. Notice verse 9: ". . . and be found in Him, not having mine own righteousness, which is of the law, but that which is through the faith of Christ, the righteousness which is of God by faith."

Any righteousness other than the imputed righteousness of Christ is mere legalism. It is incapable of saving anyone. More than that, it is an affront to God—as if we were to offer Him soiled rags and expect Him to applaud us for doing so. That kind of legalism is spiritually fatal.

How Is Christian Obedience Different from Legalism?

It has become fashionable in some circles to pin the label of "legalism" on any teaching that stresses obedience to Christ. At the beginning of this chapter I quoted someone who stated that "the whole difference between legalism and true Christianity" is sewn up in the issue of whether we view obedience as a duty.

Biblically, there is no basis for such thinking. The Christian is still obligated to obey God, even though we know our obedience in no sense provides grounds for our justification. That is precisely why our obedience should be motivated primarily by gratitude to and love for the Lord. We are free from the threat of eternal condemnation (Romans 8:1). We are free from the law of sin and death (verse 2), and empowered by God's grace both to will and to do of His good pleasure (Philippians 2:13). We have every reason to obey joyfully—and no true Christian will ever think of obedience as something optional.

We are not under law, but under grace. Far from being a manifesto for antinomianism or an authorization for licentious behavior, however, that important truth teaches us that both our justification and our obedience must properly be grounded in Christ and what He has done for us, rather than in ourselves and what we do for God.

The doctrine of justification by faith therefore provides the highest, purest incentive for Christian obedience. As Paul wrote to the Romans, the mercies God displays in our justification provide all the reason we need to yield ourselves to Him as living sacrifices (Romans 12:1). Freed from the penalty of the law—loosed from the threat of condemnation for our disobedience—we are thus empowered by grace to surrender to God in a way we were powerless to do as unbelievers. And that is why the Christian life is continually portrayed in Scrip-ture as a life of obedience.

No, obedience is not an issue of legalism, as many in our libertine age would have us believe; it is an issue of love—loving God as He commands us to do by doing what He commands—and we do so because we love Him so.

[This material was first published in 1996 in the book *Trust and Obey: Obedience and the Christian*, published by Soli Deo Gloria Publications. It is used by permission of Ligonier Ministries.]

Zealous But Not Legalistic
Joel R. Beeke

The plant known as the rosary pea (*abrus precatorius*) is an aggressive plant, even invasive if introduced to a new environment. It produces attractive red and black seeds a quarter of an inch across. They are used in necklaces or other ornaments in some parts of the world. Yet its seeds contain abrin, an extremely dangerous toxin. If chewed or sucked on and then swallowed, one seed can kill an adult.

Legalistic zeal is like the rosary pea: aggressive, attractive, and deadly. John Flavel (1628–1691) warned that an "abundance of precious souls perish in the Christianized and professing world" through "formal hypocrisy in religion, and zeal about the externals of worship."[1] The world is full of religion that produces a great mass of branches and leaves—outwardly beautiful in form, but bearing no fruit of the Spirit. It is worthless[2] in the sight of God and poisonous to the souls of men.

It may be religion driven by zeal for beautiful buildings and rituals. Think of the Pharisees: "Men that honored the dead, and persecuted the living saints; that reverenced the material temple, and destroyed the living temples."[3] Or it may be religion energized by zeal for sound doctrine without love for Christ: "How many are there that hate doctrinal errors, who yet perish by practical ones? Who hate a false doctrine, but, in the meantime, perish by a false heart?"[4] Or it may be religion fueled by zeal

---

[1] John Flavel, *A Treatise of the Soul of Man,* in *The Works of John Flavel* (1820; repr., Edinburgh: Banner of Truth, 1968), 3:214. Many thanks to Paul Smalley for his assistance on this chapter.

[2] "In vain do they worship me" (Mark 7:7).

[3] Flavel, *A Treatise of the Soul of Man,* 3:215.

[4] *Flavel, A Treatise of the Soul of Man, 3:215.*

against corruptions in public worship, yet lacking the power of godliness. Flavel said, "Nothing is more common than to find men hot and zealous against false worship, whilst their hearts are as cold as a stone in the vitals and essentials of true religion."[5]

Whatever form it takes, legalistic zeal infects the soul with a dangerous fever even while it gives the appearance of being on fire for God. Christ taught that just as a tree will bear fruit according to its nature, so our works flow from our hearts. So it is with zeal. Gracious zeal bears good fruit as surely as an apple tree produces apples. Legalistic zeal is a noxious plant, whether it exists as a small seed or a large bush full of poisonous berries. It is dangerous not just when it grows up to full size, but from its smallest beginnings. Legalism contains viciousness in its spiritual DNA. It is of a different nature than true godly zeal.

What are the distinctive marks of this destructive counterfeit? How can we avoid them? This chapter will draw out biblical warnings against legalistic zeal, first against its bitter roots described in Romans 10:1–4, and, second, against its poisonous fruits in Galatians 1:13–14.

The Bitter Roots of Legalistic Zeal

The Apostle Paul warned us of the very real danger of legalistic zeal in Romans 10:1–4: "Brethren, my heart's desire and prayer to God for Israel is that they might be saved. For I bear them record that they have a zeal of God, but not according to knowledge. For they being ignorant of God's righteousness, and going about to establish their own righteousness, have not submitted themselves unto the righteousness of God. For Christ is the end of the law for righteousness to every one that believeth."

Here Paul describes people who have a zeal for God. They have a religious passion. They work with energy and diligence. Yet their zeal sets them *against* both God and Christ. He speaks here of many of his kinsmen among the people of Israel (Ro-

---

[5] Flavel, *A Treatise of the Soul of Man,* 3:216.

mans 9:3–4). It burdened Paul's heart that, though they had so many advantages as Israelites, externally in covenant with God (Romans 9:1–5), nevertheless their zealous pursuit of a righteousness of their own had hardened their hearts against Christ and blinded them to the gospel offer of justification ("God's righteousness") by faith alone. They were religious and zealous, but not saved.

We have no ground to boast in ourselves as believers, in contrast to the Jews who rejected Christ; instead, we should fear (Romans 11:20). What do we have that we have not received? What are we apart from God's grace? Paul warns that the Lord will break our branch off of His tree just as He broke off theirs— if we fall into the same trap. This legalism is not an ethnic trait or a cultural tendency. It is a human problem, something rooted in fallen human nature. It should disturb and sober us. Where does this legalistic zeal come from? Paul's statement gives us two answers.

1. The Legalistic Pursuit of Self-Righteousness

Paul said that they were "going about to establish their own righteousness." Their zeal was a passion to prove themselves right before God and men. Self-righteousness is the great fire that heats to boiling the religion of fallen men. There is no limit to the desire of fallen humans to show themselves righteous, especially in comparison to others. Paul rebuked such people for judging and condemning others while they commit the same sins (Romans 2:1–3). Our Lord confronted those "which trusted in themselves that they were righteous, and despised others," rebuking them for their confidence before God that they are "not as other men are" (Luke 18:9, 11).

The gospel leaves no place for boasting in man.[6] The many warnings in the New Testament against such boasting show that proud sinners have an insatiable desire to glory in themselves. We especially crave reasons to boast in our righteousness. We

---

[6] Isaiah 2:22; Jeremiah 9:23–24; 1 Corinthians 1:29–31; Galatians 6:14; Ephesians 2:9.

boast of our theological acumen, our high moral standards, and our many religious duties and church activities, even as we dishonor God and transgress His law (Romans 2:17–24). In the end we would prefer to accuse the righteous Lord of wrongdoing than to accept the guilt that our own sins bring (Romans 3:3–6; Genesis 3:12).

True zeal pants after God's glory, not our own. William Plumer (1802–1880) wrote: "True zeal is not light without heat; yet it is modest. If God be glorified and His cause advanced, it is willing to remain unnoticed. It is ready to contend earnestly, but not bitterly, for the truth. If it falls into error, it is not incorrigible."[7] True zeal is not a prejudice that blinds us to correction.

Sadly, our fallen nature lusts after the admiration and praise of men, wanting to be seen of them and be highly esteemed for our record of perfect attendance at church or the money we give to Christian causes. Christ drove a wedge between true godliness and such hypocrisy by warning: "Take heed that ye do not your alms before men, to be seen of them: otherwise ye have no reward of your Father which is in heaven" (Mattehew 6:1). Our hearts most naturally delight in outward works of religion, for they alone are seen by people (Matthew 23:25–28). Even evangelism and missions can be driven by a lust for glory among men.[8] Thus Paul discriminated between true believers and the wicked by saying in Romans 2:29: "He is a Jew, which is one inwardly; and circumcision is that of the heart, in the spirit, and not in the letter; whose praise is not of men, but of God."

Here is the first bitter root of legalistic zeal: our wholehearted commitment to our self-righteousness. How do we put off this innate and pervasive passion for our own righteousness? How can we be zealous for the Lord without falling into this natural legalism?

---

[7] William S. Plumer, *Vital Godliness: A Treatise on Experimental and Practical Piety* (1864; repr., Harrisonburg, Va.: Sprinkle, 1993), 558.
[8] Matthew 23:15; Galatians 6:13; Philippians 1:15.

We must be zealous for the Lord, but with the zeal of repentance (Romans 2:4). Our Lord joined the two together when He
said, "be zealous therefore, and repent" (Revelation 3:19). Zeal
must begin with renouncing and forsaking our own sins. Richard
Greenham (c. 1542–1594) wrote: "True zeal beginneth in ourselves, and taketh his proceeding to others. For never can that
man be zealous to others, which never knew to be zealous to
himself. . . . True zeal casteth the first stone at ourselves."[9] There
is no true zeal for the Lord that does not come from brokenness
of heart, self-abhorrence, and turning away from our own sins.
No one can hunger for righteousness until he sees himself as a
poor beggar (Matthew 5:3, 6). Godly zeal is a fruit of godly sor-
row, the kind of grief that produces repentance unto salvation (2
Corinthians 7:10–11).

Ironically, if we would avoid legalism, then we must make
zealous use of God's law. But we must use it rightly. We must
refrain from picking the specks from the eyes of others until we
first remove the great shafts of wood from our own (Matthew
7:5). We must look into the perfect law of liberty and continue
therein, turning from sin to become doers of the Word (James
1:22–25). We must let the Ten Commandments and their appli-
cations search us thoroughly, until we fall on our faces before
God.[10] Then we will be ready to deal with the other bitter root
of legalistic zeal.

2. *The Legalistic Rejection of Divine Righteousness*

Paul wrote in Romans 10:2 that "they have a zeal of God,
but not according to knowledge. . . . being ignorant of the God's
righteousness." The righteousness of God here refers to God's
saving work by the submission of Christ to the law, including

---

[9] *The Workes of the Reverend and Faithfvll Servant of Iesvs Christ M. Richard
Greenham.... The Second Edition* (London: by Felix Kingston, for Ralph
Iacson, 1599), 113–114.
[10] An excellent resource for applying the Ten Commandments is the Westminster Larger Catechism, Q. 91–152.

submission to its penalty of death (Romans 10:4).[11] It is the gift of righteousness apart from our works, counted to all who believe in Christ, though in the strict judgment of the law they are ungodly (Romans 4:3–8). I am speaking here of the gospel of justification by faith in Christ alone. These people, zealous for God, nevertheless did not know the good news of the righteousness of God that is by faith in Christ Jesus, and were damned for it.

We must not imagine that they were "ignorant" in the sense of having no exposure to the gospel. The gospel had gone forth in Israel just as surely as the sunshine proclaims God's glory to all the earth (Romans 10:18; cf. Psalm 19:1–6). The Lord exclaimed, "All day long I have stretched forth My hands unto a disobedient and gainsaying people" (Romans 10:21).

Their problem was not a lack of information, but hardness of heart. They "have not submitted themselves unto the righteousness of God" (Romans 10:3). Just as self-righteousness is the passion of proud sinners, so God's righteousness is the object of their willful blindness. We do not know Christ's righteousness because we do not want to know it. It takes a mighty work of the Holy Spirit to convince us of our sin and our need of Christ's righteousness (John 16:8–11). Apart from the Spirit's work we are enemies of the gospel, inwardly resolving with unconverted Paul, that "I ought to do many things contrary to the name of Jesus of Nazareth" (Acts 26:9).

Inward resistance to the gospel of justification is not limited to unbelievers. Believers often slip into denying the gospel in practical ways. Astonishingly, even Peter, a seasoned gospel preacher, was rebuked by Paul on one occasion because Peter and Barnabas "walked not uprightly according to the truth of the gospel" (Galatians 2:14). He had failed to treat all Christians, Gentiles as well as Jews, as people justified totally by the righteousness of Christ. In this instance Peter appeared zealous for the

---

[11] See Romans 1:17; 3:21–26; 5:17–18; 2 Corinthians 5:21; Philippians 3:9.

Old Testament laws, but he was actually driven by the fear of man to compromise his faith and love (Galatians 2:12). Legalism often arises from the fear of man.

Legalism also creeps into believers by way of doubts about the gospel. Our experiential knowledge of the gospel may be weak. We may understand that we are justified by Christ's righteousness alone, but we have an experiential ignorance, a practical blind spot, that leads us to live as if under a covenant of works. We might be zealous, but our zeal might spring from a false sense that we must somehow keep ourselves right with God by doing more for Him. Guilt is a harsh master and it may produce results. But it will never produce comfort, peace, love, or a good conscience. Paul reminds believers: "For ye have not received the spirit of bondage again to fear; but ye have received the Spirit of adoption, whereby we cry, Abba, Father" (Romans 8:15).

This is the second bitter root of legalistic zeal: resistance against God's gift of righteousness in Christ. How can we dig up this root and cut it off?

By grace, we must continue to exercise faith in the Lord Jesus Christ as our only righteousness before God. As we walk with God, we must do so trusting that "the blood of Jesus Christ his Son cleanseth us from all sin" (1 John 1:7). We must not try to hide our sins, deny our sins, or try to atone for our sins. Who can repay those "ten thousand talents"? For that is what we owe— more than what a hundred lifetimes of hard labor could repay (Matthew 18:24, 26).

Instead, we must confess our sins to God and believe that "He is faithful and just to forgive us our sins" (1 John 1:9). Why *just*? How can justice move God to forgive sin? God's justice compels Him to keep His promise, in this case, to forgive and to cleanse. So the promise is sure, and can be relied on, for peace of conscience and assurance of pardon.

We must constantly couple our confession of sins to a conscious reliance upon our "advocate with the Father, Jesus Christ the righteous; and He is the propitiation for our sins" (1 John

2:1–2). His justice-satisfying and wrath-appeasing sacrifice guarantees that now, as He intercedes for His people, God's very justice will certify their full forgiveness.

In a word, the gospel must become our daily bread. Having begun in grace we must continue by grace. We must constantly preach Christ's righteousness to our self-righteous souls, and renounce the sinful quest for a righteousness of our own. That is the only way to fight back against legalistic zeal and mortify it so that it cannot produce its bitter results in our lives.

The Poisonous Fruits of Legalistic Zeal

For the Apostle Paul, legalistic zeal was not a theory; it was his past history. When he wrote of the unbelieving Jews in Romans 10, he did not do so as an outsider, but as one remembering what he once was. He describes his pre-conversion experience in Galatians 1:13–14: "For ye have heard of my conversation [conduct] in time past in the Jews' religion, how that beyond measure I persecuted the church of God, and wasted it; and profited in the Jews' religion above many my equals in mine own nation, being more exceedingly zealous of the traditions of my fathers."

Paul was zealous, literally a "super-abundant zealot." Paul, or Saul as he was then known, pursued his religious goals with fervor far beyond that of the average Jew, even "beyond measure." Such energy and dedication is admirable. He puts many Christians to shame for our half-hearted, sleepy-headed religion. William Perkins (1558–1602) said: "That which Paul did in his [pre-conversion] religion, we must do in ours. The good things that we are to do, we must do them with all our might (Ecclesiastes 9:10)."[12]

But his zeal produced remarkably ugly and harmful fruit. It was not enough for him to approve of the murder of Stephen

---

[12] William Perkins, *A Commentary on Galatians,* ed. Gerald T. Sheppard (1617; facsimile repr. with introductions, New York: Pilgrim Press, 1989), 37.

(Acts 8:1); he must set out on his own campaign to persecute the church, "breathing out threatenings and slaughter" (Acts 8:3, 9:1). Legalistic zeal is not just going overboard in religion. Legalistic zeal is poisonous in its very nature, and the tree shows itself in its fruit.

Violent Hatred of Other Parties

Paul confessed, "beyond measure I persecuted the church of God, and wasted it." We read in Acts 8:3, that "as for Saul, he made havock of the church, entering into every house, and haling men and women committed them to prison." Paul later said, "I persecuted this way unto the death, binding and delivering into prisons both men and women" (Acts 22:4); and he voiced his approval when they were put to death (Acts 26:10). He did this out of his religious zeal (Phil. 3:6).

Paul had such dedication to this task that it was not enough for him to persecute the church in Jerusalem: "And I punished them oft in every synagogue, and compelled them to blaspheme; and being exceedingly mad against them, I persecuted them even unto strange cities" (Acts 26:11). He went to the high priest, "breathing out threatenings and slaughter against the disciples of the Lord," and obtained authorization to extend his campaigning to Damascus (Acts 9:1–2).

Why did Paul so violently attack the church without mercy or compassion? In his own words, he was "zealous toward God" (Acts 22:3). This should sober us and cause us to search our souls. Here is a man who worshiped the true God, not a false or pagan deity. He knew the Holy Scriptures, probably better than many Christian ministers today (Acts 22:3). In some respects he was more theologically orthodox than the liberals of the day, for he was a Pharisee holding to the hope of the resurrection, not a Sadducee (Acts 26:5–8; Matt. 22:23). So he was zealous for God. Nevertheless, his zeal was only a flame of murderous, intolerant hatred.

Such legalistic zeal is far from the love of God. Plumer wrote of true, Christian zeal, that "for peace it will give up everything but truth and a good conscience. It wars not after [or according to] the flesh. It rejects carnal weapons. It is full of courtesy, candor [honest sincerity], and kindness. It forbears. It forgives. It pities. It yields to reasonable arguments and suggestions. It is not obstinate. It hates malice. It loves mercy."[13]

God's people too easily become swept up in a zeal that is driven by the wrath of man instead of the love of God. Someone might object that Paul was an unbeliever driven along by hatred against Christ. But even the disciples of Christ can succumb to it. When a village of Samaria would not welcome Jesus, His disciples said, "Lord, wilt thou that we command fire to come down from heaven, and consume them, even as Elias did?" Christ rebuked them, "Ye know not what manner of spirit ye are of. For the Son of man is not come to destroy men's lives, but to save them" (Luke 9:54–56). They were zealous for Christ, but not according to the Spirit of Christ.

Again, someone might object that we are not murderers like Saul. But legalistic zeal does not always provoke men to destroy others; sometimes they simply try to shut them out or shut them down. John, one of the "sons of thunder," exhibited this party spirit when he said, "Master, we saw one casting out devils in thy name; and we forbad him, because he followeth not with us." Christ answered, "Forbid him not: for he that is not against us is for us" (Luke 9:49–50). How sad it is when some of Christ's servants try to hinder other servants of Christ because they "followeth not with us." A sectarian or party spirit has too often divided the churches.

How poisonous is the fruit of legalistic zeal! It is not the fruit of the Spirit: "love, joy, peace, longsuffering, gentleness, goodness, faith, meekness, temperance" (Gal. 5:22–23). Instead such zeal produces the horrifying works of the flesh: "hatred, variance, emulations, wrath, strife, seditions, heresies, envyings, murders" (Gal. 5:20–21).

---

[13] Plumer, *Vital Godliness*, 558.

Such zeal often cloaks itself in impressive wisdom. It can quote Bible verses and respected teachers to support its positions. By their knowledge of theology and skill in debate legalists can make other people feel foolish and ignorant. But their wisdom is "earthly" and "devilish"—of Satan himself—as is evident from the "envying and strife" it produces in the heart and "confusion and every evil work" it brings forth in the life (James 3:14–16). Legalistic zeal seems wise, "but the wisdom that is from above is first pure, then peaceable, gentle, and easy to be intreated, full of mercy and good fruits, without partiality, and without hypocrisy. And the fruit of righteousness is sown in peace of them that make peace" (vv. 17–18).

Therefore we must guard our hearts for from them flow the issues of life (Prov. 4:23). We must keep watch not only over what we say and do, but also the spirit in which we do it. Perhaps a brother has fallen into sin or error. We must correct him. But do we do it "in the spirit of meekness"? Is our sincere goal to "restore such an one"? Are we seeking to bear "one another's burdens, and so fulfill the law of Christ"? If we are not, then even if we think we are something, we deceive ourselves and are nothing (Gal. 6:1–3; cf. 1 Cor. 13:2). We must do the right things for the right reasons, and in the right way.

True zeal will not lead us to wrathful hatred toward sinners, but broken-hearted grief over their sin. The psalmist wrote, "Rivers of waters run down mine eyes, because they keep not thy law. . . . My zeal hath consumed me, because mine enemies have forgotten thy words" (Ps. 119:136, 139). Jeremiah was deeply offended by Israel's sins, yet exclaimed, "Oh that my head were waters, and mine eyes a fountain of tears, that I might weep day and night for the slain of the daughter of my people!" (Jer. 9:1). True zeal makes us like Christ, who wept over Jerusalem for the judgment coming upon them even as He anticipated His own crucifixion.

Guard yourself against the divisive impulses of legalistic zeal. Is the church divided into parties? Let us avoid clinging to the names of men, and boast in Christ and Him crucified (1 Cor.

1:10–18). Have some fallen into heresies? Then let the servant of God correct them with gentleness and patience, trusting in sovereign grace to grant repentance (2 Tim. 2:24–25). Let us love our enemies and pray for them (Matt. 5:44). In all things let us not direct attention to mere men, but present ourselves as servants and direct attention to Christ. Unless we labor to constantly maintain Scripture as our only divine rule and Christ as our only sovereign king, we will produce hatred and the other poisonous fruit of legalistic zeal.

Commitment to Man's Traditions

When Paul spoke of his former legalistic zeal in Judaism, in addition to his violent hatred against the church he said that he was "exceedingly zealous of the traditions of my fathers." This too is a fruit of legalistic zeal: an entrenched commitment to human tradition. Paul warns us in Colossians 2:8 to "beware lest any man spoil you through philosophy and vain deceit, after the tradition of men, after the rudiments of the world, and not after Christ."

The word "spoil" here communicates a man conquering you and taking you captive, as the spoils of war. Human wisdom is enthralling and captivates sinful hearts. It seems spiritual. It judges people by rules and duties that God does not command (Colossians 2:16); it exalts in false humility and mysticism (Colossians 2:18); it puts up a show of asceticism and man-made forms of worship that have no power to overcome sin (Colossians 2:20–23). In all its various manifestations, mere human tradition fails to point men to Christ as our righteousness and head by whose death and exaltation we are complete (Colossians 2:6–15, 17, 19, 20; 3:1–4).

Our Lord Jesus was specifically criticized by the Pharisees and scribes for not following "the tradition of the elders" (Mark 7:5). Christ rebuked them, "Well hath Esaias prophesied of you hypocrites, as it is written, This people honoureth Me with their lips, but their heart is far from Me. Howbeit in vain do they worship Me, teaching for doctrines the commandments of men"

(Mark 7:6–7). By investing supreme authority in human traditions, they effectively nullified the Word of God (Mark 7:8–9).
In this way, human tradition serves our great passion for self-
righteousness, for it grants us a cover of false piety to hide our
neglect of God's commandments.

Tradition can be a blessing to the church if by it we pass
down to future generations the doctrine and commandments of
Holy Scripture (2 Timothy 2:2). Paul called his own teaching
"traditions" in the sense of an authoritative teaching to be cher-
ished and practiced by the church (2 Thessalonians 2:15; 3:6)
from generation to generation. By our confessions of faith and
catechisms and orders of worship, each church shields its elder-
ship from false teachers (Titus 1:9) and guards the good deposit
of sound doctrine for future generations to embrace in faith and
love (2 Timothy 1:13–14). But the traditions of the church have
no divine authority to bind the conscience except insofar as they
faithfully conform to the written Word of God.

Paul wrote to Timothy that he must persevere in *biblical* tradition, saying, "But continue thou in the things which thou hast
learned and hast been assured of, knowing of whom thou hast
learned them; and that from a child thou hast known the holy
scriptures, which are able to make thee wise unto salvation
through faith which is in Christ Jesus" (2 Timothy 3:14–15). For
the Scriptures, unlike the words of fallible human beings, are totally reliable and entirely profitable, for all the Bible is breathed
forth by the Spirit of God (2 Timothy 3:16).

We must willingly subject our beliefs and practices to the
scrutiny of Holy Scripture. The principle of *sola Scriptura* (Scripture alone) stood at the heart of the Reformation. The church at
that time had accumulated centuries of unbiblical traditions in
doctrine, worship, church government, and daily Christian life.
The Bible served as a razor to shave away human additions, resulting in the Reformed church. But, human nature being what it
is, we constantly face the temptation to elevate our traditions to
divine status. We must humble ourselves when someone challenges our convictions and always ask, "What do the Scriptures

say?" This also demands that the church teach the Bible to each new generation, and not simply rely upon its traditions.

Since legalistic tradition amplifies some aspect of God's Word while neglecting other aspects, *sola Scriptura* also means maintaining biblical priorities. The Pharisees were meticulous tithers (a good thing), but neglected the larger matters of the law, such as justice and love. Christ accused them of straining a gnat out of their food, but swallowing a camel (Matthew 23:23–24), or, as we would say, majoring in the minors while minoring in the majors.

The Lord has told us the great priorities: the law of *loving God with all our hearts and loving our neighbor as ourselves,* and the gospel that *God saves sinners through Christ by a Spirit-worked faith* (Matthew 22:37–40; 1 Corinthians 15:1–10; 12:3). We must keep ourselves and our churches focused on these central matters, and it will protect us from the ugliness of legalism. If we are zealous for love and the gospel of Christ, then our zeal will please God and reveal His beauty to the world.

Keeping our focus on the heart of the law and gospel will also protect us from falling into Peter's trap: a mistaken separatism from other believers (Galatians 2:11–14). This is a sensitive matter, for we must also beware of the opposite error of an ecumenism that is too accommodating. We must separate ourselves from the sins of the world and from idolatrous worship (2 Corinthians 6:14–18). We should have no fellowship with heretical teachers who deny the gospel (2 John 7, 9–11). We must also separate ourselves from impenitent, professing Christians placed under church discipline for their wrongdoing and hardness of heart (1 Corinthians 5).

But there is a prideful kind of separatism that the Scriptures condemn (3 John 9–10). Samuel Ward (1577–1640) wrote against wrongful separatism: "For who would not suspect such zeal, which condemns all reformed churches, and refuseth communion with such as they themselves confess to be Christians, and consequently such as have communion with Christ?"[14] Here we must search our hearts and measure our actions by the Scriptures lest we fall into the error of Roger Williams (c. 1603–1683), who began as an advocate for religious liberty and tolerance, but ultimately separated from all visible churches because none was totally pure.

Different Christians have come to different conclusions about where to draw the line on separation. We must respect these differences regarding separation. But we must all embrace the fundamental calling to cherish unity in the body of Christ (Ephesians 4:3). The gospel demands that we welcome one another even if we disagree on some nonessential matters (Romans 14:1, 4). What would we do if Christ separated Himself from us until our teaching and worship were pure? Let us receive each other as Christ received us, to the glory of God (Romans 15:7). Then we will be able to speak the truth to each other in love, as iron sharpens iron, until we all attain to the unity of the faith and of the knowledge of the Son of God (Ephesians 4:13, 15).

Zeal Ignited by the Grace of Christ for the Glory of Christ

Does this mean that all zeal is legalism? Such is the opinion of worldly Christians and so-called moderates, who would allow for religion so long as it keeps in its place. But the reality is far different. There is indeed a gracious zeal, indeed a fervent zeal that God commands (Romans 12:11; Revelation 3:19). Ward said that "Christian zeal" is "a spiritual heat wrought in the heart of man by the Holy Ghost" that stirs and advances "the good affections of love, joy, hope, etc., for the best service and furtherance of God's glory," and engages a holy "hatred, anger, [and] grief" against Satan and sin.[15]

---

[14] Samuel Ward, *A Coal from the Altar*, in *Sermons* (1862; repr., Edinburgh: Banner of Truth, 1996), 76.

[15] Ward, *A Coal from the Altar*, 72.

God Himself is zealous for His glory among the nations (Isaiah 9:7; 48:11). The Lord Jesus Christ burned with zeal for the house of God (John 2:17). Knowing His love for us, we become zealous in our love for Him (Luke 7:37–50; 2 Corinthians 5:14–15). His zeal for His glory enters into us, igniting us to burn with the same imperishable love for His name.

The death of Christ produces a people who are "zealous of good works" (Titus 2:14). These are not just works of public ministry. The redeemed are zealous to fulfill their earthly vocations in a way that makes the beauty of God's truth to shine, including the domestic labors of godly mothers (Titus 2:1–10). They are zealous to obey proper authorities and to treat people with gentleness and meekness, remembering God's saving grace to them (Titus 3:1–8).

Above all, the godly man is zealous for Christ Himself. He puts no confidence in the flesh, no matter what religious privileges and attainments he might have (Philippians 3:3–7). He says with Paul, "I count all things but loss for the excellency of the knowledge of Christ Jesus my Lord" (Philippians 3:8). And therefore his life is one great pursuit of Christ, where he constantly presses on to grasp hold of the zealous One who has grasped hold of him (Philippians 3:12–14).[16]

---

[16] For an examination of godly zeal and encouragements towards it, see Joel R. Beeke and James A. La Belle, *Living Zealously* (Grand Rapids: Reformation Heritage Books, 2012).

The Plague of
Free-Will Moralism

or

How to Kill the Doctrine of Salvation by "Free Grace
Alone" by simply asserting the Pelagian Doctrine of
Free-Will Moralism!

Kenneth Gary Talbot

The term "legalism," or any variation thereof, cannot be
found in either the Old Testament or the New Testament. However, the Greek term *nomos*, which is translated as "law" has been
used as a basis for the use of the term legalism in theological lit-
erature. But even this term is often misunderstood when law is
used in connection with salvation, whether it is God's law or
man's law, pre or post regeneration. Legalism as it relates to salvation is my topic of interest in the chapter. We must first de-
termine a proper definition of the term legalism in order to
rightfully understand what we are trying to identify by the use of
this term in the context of religion, and more specifically in this
particular area of church dogma—salvation. The reason this is
important is that the majority of the professed evangelical
church today is held captive by some variation of legalism in its
doctrine of salvation. This verity of legalism is the surest means
of killing the doctrine of "salvation by free grace alone."

The term legalism in a broader context may be defined
within various frameworks, allowing it to have multiple mean-
ings depending on the nature of the subject matter. However,
we are not concerned with the broader context in which legalism

can be defined; rather the underlying principle will always emphasize "form" over "substance" in every context that it might appear. To focus upon a more definitive understanding of the term legalism in a soteriological context we can with some safety consider the term as it is usually identified in two specific dogmas in which it finds theological expression: justification and sanctification. Justification deals with the question of "how does one receive acceptance from God in salvation?" Sanctification deals with the question "how does an individual, having received acceptance from God, then maintain their salvific status with Him?" While we really need to look carefully at these questions, time and space will allow us to only deal with the first area of consideration, that of salvific justification. Yet this is not to deny the importance of sanctification because it and justification are a part the doctrine of salvation. Thus, when the allegation of legalism is made, it is most commonly found in these two realms of soteriological dogma.

From this perspective, legalism would be defined as that teaching wherein an individual is seeking to bring either the law of God or some form of works-righteousness into the doctrine of justification by faith. Either case constitutes a form of legalism because there is within that individual's system of theology some component of meritorious effort on the part of the individual which he 'must contribute' to gain acceptance with God.

Either concept is seeking justification through the means of obedience, whether it is being attributed to the law of God or by some other meritorious act wherein man can restore himself to a right standing before God. Theologically speaking, both cases are considered a "works-righteousness" salvation. By works-righteousness we mean salvation that includes human meritorious effort as a cause of redemption, without which man cannot gain salvation. Therefore, in seeking to be as precise as possible in our definition of legalism as expressed in this soteriological context, we would maintain that legalism is any attempt by man to obtain God's favor resulting in salvation. It is a contributory act of man that is necessary in order to be justified by God.

Thus, when man seeks to gain salvation through his own ability alone, apart from any action of God directly that would affect man, it is called "autosoterism."

Autosoterism is a theological perspective which maintains that, in salvation, it is human merit alone that provides the means for acceptance with God. This has historically been known as pelagianism. However, when this doctrine of pelagianism is synthesized with some aspect of God supplying a part of the salvation, this type of soteriology is referred to as semi-pelagianism. Pelagianism is based on man as the sole provider for his own salvation through some form of meritorious effort based on man's ability to gain favor and therefore achieve salvation with God; this salvation is apart from any work provided for by God. Semi-pelagianism is a combination of salvation based on one part God and one part man. Man is always considered as primary in this synergistic relationship, with God depending and waiting upon man to perform some act of contrition. Let's examine pelagianism first and then move on to the semi-pelagianism, which at first seems different from pelagianism, but in reality it is not in substance different at all.

Pelagianism is a term that historically refers to the soteriology of the ascetic monk Pelagius (AD 354—after 418), a Catholic theologian from the region of the British Isles. Pelagius opposed the doctrine of Augustine's soteriological dogma based on his doctrine of predestination. Augustine asserted that salvation was by grace "alone" and, as a result of Adam's original sin, his will was considered bound or completely suppressed by sin and therefore passive in the initial work of the Holy Spirit. Although Augustine held that justification was by grace alone, completely the work of God via the Holy Spirit, yet he believed that it was totally infused grace. Contrary to Pelagius, Augustine maintained that salvation from beginning to end was only based on the meritorious work of Christ through the grace of God. While we would not agree with the erroneous way Augustine defines salvation in relation to justification as being completely infused by the Holy Spirit (including justification), we do accept the fact that he was correct in that salvation was solely and completely a work of God's grace without one contribution from man. Thus, Augustine rightfully held that this work of regeneration by the Holy Spirit was an act of God's free grace to those who were elected before the foundation of the world in the person of Christ. It is important to note that Christ did not make a way of salvation for man, but was salvation himself. Augustine believed that St. Paul had clearly written concerning this nature of salvation as being by grace alone and not the work of man.

The Apostle Paul stated the doctrine clearly in Ephesians 1:3–14:

> Blessed be the God and Father of our Lord Jesus Christ, who has blessed us with every spiritual blessing in the heavenly places in Christ, just as He chose us in Him before the foundation of the world, that we should be holy and without blame before Him in love, having predestined us to adoption as sons by Jesus Christ to Himself, according to the good pleasure of His will, to the praise of the glory of His grace, by which He made us accepted in the Beloved. In Him we have redemption through His blood, the forgiveness of sins, according to the riches of His grace which He made to abound toward us in all wisdom and prudence, having made known to us the mystery of His will, according to His good pleasure which He purposed in Himself, that in the dispensation of the fullness of the times He might gather together in one all things in Christ, both which are in heaven and which are on earth—in Him. In Him also we have obtained an inheritance, being predestined according to the purpose of Him who works all things according to the counsel of His will, that we who first trusted in Christ should be to the praise of His glory. In Him you also trusted, after you heard the word of truth, the gospel of your salvation; in whom also, having believed, you were sealed with the Holy Spirit of

> promise, who is the guarantee of our inheritance
> until the redemption of the purchased possession,
> to the praise of His glory.

A closer examination of this text will be very beneficial in our understanding of salvation as being an act of God's grace alone. St. Paul writes: "Blessed be the God and Father of our Lord Jesus Christ, who has blessed us with every spiritual blessing in the heavenly places in Christ." First note that we have the triune God involved in the salvation of man. We have "God and Father," the "Lord Jesus Christ," and the "spiritual blessings" which refers to the application of the Holy Spirit as the efficient cause. This particular text has been referred to as the Covenant of Redemption, the reason being that it reveals the will of God among the three persons of the Godhead thereby expressing purpose and intent of God prior to the creation of anything that exists. Further, this also is an expression of the economy of salvation— God chooses a people, the Son of God redeems those chosen by the Father, and the Holy Spirit applies that redemption to them. In this immediate context we are told that those "spiritual blessings" are in the "heavenly places in Christ." This statement is a reference to God the Son having ascended unto the Father, which was symbolic of the Father's approval that Christ's work had provided all the necessary means of salvation in His death, burial, and resurrection. Wherein Christ was told to sit at the right hand of God—another symbolism that asserts approval of the completed work and the vesting of one who had been given authority. Christ's work of salvation was accepted by the Father as fully atoning for sin; this was proof that Jesus Christ is the High Priest of His people in the satisfaction of their sins before God the Father. Therefore, to state that our salvation is in "heavenly places" means that "positionally" we are redeemed in Christ. In this way we are then considered fully justified, that is, legally restored to a right standing before God the Father. However, the completion of salvation's outworking has not yet reached its full intention in glorification. We have yet to be given our resurrection body, which is a part of God's promise in salvation. The apostle continues: "just as He (God the Father) chose us (unilateral election of those who will be identified in time as believers) in Him (Christ) before the foundation of the world (before creation), that we (elect/believers) should be holy (righteous) and without blame (pardoned for our sins) before Him (the Father)."

Our salvation is not bilateral—meaning consisting of a contribution on the part of both God and man—rather, it is unilateral. It is salvation completely supplied, meaning not only does Christ atone for sin, but atonement also comes with all that is necessary for man to actually respond to the gospel. Therefore, God gives His Son to atone for sin, and then He also grants all things necessary for us to respond to the calling of the Father in salvation to His Son through the means of proclaiming the gospel. Considering this we say that salvation is all of grace, plus nothing (from man) and minus nothing (from God). Paul continues by stating, "in love" which is the motivating grace of God toward those chosen as the Father's elect. In love, God "predestined us," that is, God the Father determined to bring His elect/believers to salvation at our appointed times throughout history. Then Paul adds that the Father's purpose of predestinating us is "to adoption as sons." This means that God legally places us in the family of God as His children. The reason for this being necessary in salvation is this: if God had only pardoned us from our sins, that would have simply placed us back into the same circumstance that Adam had been prior to the fall. Therefore, we would have been required to make a choice just like Adam as to whether we continue serving God or not. This is the principle behind pelagianism.

However, God does not save man partially. When God saves men, He provides full salvation. Therefore, we are not returned to the position of Adam in the Garden prior to the fall, with each man left to make a decision like Adam at an age of accountability. Rather, when original sin is eliminated, we are not only pardoned, but we are also placed in the family of God as sons or children by a legal act of adoption. By this action of adoption we

are given eternal surety as to our heavenly status as being a child
or son of God. How was this accomplished? Paul brings all this
together in this text by pointing out that our salvation was actually secured "by Jesus Christ" who does not make a *way* of salvation, but is *actually* salvation.

Further, Paul makes it clear that this work of the Son in salvation was to "bring" the Father's elect "to Himself," according
to the good pleasure of His (God the Father's) will. This is a gracious bestowing of the salvation accomplished by Christ's
atonement because it pleased God the Father. This, we are told,
was according to what He had determined before the foundation
of the world. Such a salvation ensures that His promise that cannot be broken was fully filled or brought to pass. In Hebrew
6:13–20 the Apostle Paul assures us that the promise given to
Abraham precedes the giving of the Law. God had promised salvation by the mediation of His Son prior to the giving of the
Law. Paul writes:

> For when God made a promise to Abraham, be-
> cause He could swear by no one greater, He swore
> by Himself, saying, 'Surely blessing I will bless you,
> and multiplying I will multiply you.' And so, after
> he had patiently endured, he obtained the prom-
> ise. For men indeed swear by the greater, and an
> oath for confirmation is for them an end of all dis-
> pute. Thus God, determining to show more abun-
> dantly to the heirs of promise the immutability of
> His counsel, confirmed it by an oath, that by two
> immutable things, in which it is impossible for
> God to lie, we might have strong consolation, who
> have fled for refuge to lay hold of the hope set be-
> fore us. This hope we have as an anchor of the
> soul, both sure and steadfast, and which enters the
> Presence behind the veil, where the forerunner has
> entered for us, even Jesus, having become High
> Priest forever according to the order of
> Melchizedek.

This is further confirmed by Paul's statement in Galatians 3:13–20 wherein he makes it clear that Christ is the "promised seed" spoken of to Abraham in the covenant that God made with Him. It is the same promise God gave in Genesis 3:15. The promise of salvation is likened unto a covenant, and the binder of the covenant is God and Jesus Christ, in whom the chosen of God are elected. Paul states in his letter to the Galatians:

> Christ has redeemed us from the curse of the law, having become a curse for us (for it is written, "Cursed is everyone who hangs on a tree"), that the blessing of Abraham might come upon the Gentiles in Christ Jesus, that we might receive the promise of the Spirit through faith. Brethren, I speak in the manner of men: Though it is only a man's covenant, yet if it is confirmed, no one annuls or adds to it. Now to Abraham and his Seed were the promises made. He does not say, "And to seeds," as of many, but as of one, "And to your Seed," who is Christ. And this I say, that the law, which was four hundred and thirty years later, cannot annul the covenant that was confirmed before by God in Christ, that it should make the promise of no effect. For if the inheritance is of the law, it is no longer of promise; but God gave it to Abraham by promise. What purpose then does the law serve? It was added because of transgressions, till the Seed should come to whom the promise was made; and it was appointed through angels by the hand of a mediator. Now a mediator does not mediate for one only, but God is one.

Salvation is a covenantal promise that God has sworn to Himself that He will provide all things necessary to ensure the salvation of His chosen people, a salvation that can never be lost! Salvation was granted "in Christ" based on the promise of God Himself. That promise cannot be broken because the promise is from God who does not lie and cannot change His mind as to what He eternally decreed. If this is not true of God, then He can never be trusted in anything that He promises, because they are only empty promises. Now this explains the next statement given in this text of Ephesians where Paul states that all of this was done "to the praise of the glory of His (God the Father's) grace, by which He (God the Father) made us accepted in the Beloved (Jesus Christ)." Again consider the nature of our salvation. "We" were "made," says Paul, "accepted in the Beloved," that is in Christ. This "acceptance" was the basis of our "justification." The elect in Christ are alone justified by Christ's work. It alone assures us of our acceptance with God the Father. Paul continues, "In Him (Jesus Christ) we have redemption through His blood (salvation by sacrifice)." This is the substitutionary atonement for our sins. It is Christ's righteousness alone; it is called an alien righteousness because it is not our righteousness that accounts for our sins. Because Christ was sinless, He is the payment for our sins (the necessary sacrifice), and we therefore affirm that our sins were "imputed or accounted" to Him. His righteousness being "imputed" or "given on account of our sins," this we call the doctrine of double imputation.

This is why we cannot contribute anything to gain acceptance with God the Father. What is included in this redemption? Paul states it is "the forgiveness of sins, according to the riches of His grace which He made to abound toward us in all wisdom and prudence." Our forgiveness of sin is God's work in Christ. All that Christ has accomplished is the demonstration of the riches of God's grace that abounds to us as the "wisdom and prudence of God." Thus, Paul states this is essential to God "having made known to us (elect/believers) the mystery of His will according to His (God the Father's) good pleasure which He (God the Father) purposed in Himself." This has now been revealed in its fullness, unlike the prior era (Old Testament) wherein the promise was only given in copy and shadow in the Law of Moses.

This determinative act of salvation was the Father's plan, and it was pleasing and predetermined by His sovereign will to bring it to pass in Christ for this reason: "that in the dispensation of the fullness of the times (end of history) He (God the Father) might gather together in one all things in Christ, both which are in heaven and which are on earth in Him." The purpose of God, in decreeing all these things in His eternal plan, was that, at the end of redemptive history, He might gather all of the elect throughout history that have been chosen in Christ, thereby bringing them to the final reality of His Covenant promise, resurrection from the dead into their final eternal estate. Paul says in Romans 8:12–25:

> Therefore, brethren, we are debtors — not to the flesh, to live according to the flesh. For if you live according to the flesh you will die; but if by the Spirit you put to death the deeds of the body, you will live. For as many as are led by the Spirit of God, these are sons of God. For you did not receive the spirit of bondage again to fear, but you received the Spirit of adoption by whom we cry out, "Abba, Father." The Spirit Himself bears witness with our spirit that we are children of God, and if children, then heirs — heirs of God and joint heirs with Christ, if indeed we suffer with Him, that we may also be glorified together. For I consider that the sufferings of this present time are not worthy to be compared with the glory which shall be revealed in us. For the earnest expectation of the creation eagerly waits for the revealing of the sons of God. For the creation was subjected to futility, not willingly, but because of Him who subjected it in hope; because the creation itself also will be delivered from the bondage of corruption into the glorious liberty of the children of God. For we know that the whole creation groans and labors with birth pangs together until now. Not only that, but we also who have the first fruits of the Spirit, even we ourselves groan within ourselves, eagerly waiting for the adoption, the re-

demption of our body. For we were saved in this hope, but hope that is seen is not hope; for why does one still hope for what he sees? But if we hope for what we do not see, we eagerly wait for it with perseverance.

Therefore, Paul is expressing this very same point in our Ephesians text (Ephesians 1:3–14), saying that those who are alive on earth when He (Christ) returns again, with the elect who have already died throughout history, will descend with Him. Paul then adds a fuller expression of this when he states: "In Him (Jesus Christ) also we have obtained an inheritance (eternal life in a resurrected body) being predestined (determined by God's plan) according to the purpose of Him who works all things according to the counsel of His will, that we who first trusted in Christ should be to the praise of His glory."

We have been granted everything as being "positionally" completed as to our state in our salvation—regeneration, justification, adoption, and sanctification. All of this is based on the meritorious work of Christ alone through His atoning works in His death, burial, and resurrection, and ascension. This is precisely what salvation of the elect is—by grace alone, through Christ alone, by the instrument of faith alone. All of this is a gift of the Father to the elect by the regenerating work of the Holy Spirit while we were still bound in sin and condemned before God as lawless creatures. We were legally separated from God as breakers of His law in Adam's original sin, which resulted in our own actual sins from our birth onward. Paul says that God therefore had predetermined these things according to His own wisdom whereby it will to come to pass throughout the history of the world to those who are the elect of the Father.

Paul concludes this exhortation by stating that "In Him you also trusted," believed God and embraced His Son Jesus the Christ. This, he says, happened, "after you heard the word of truth, the gospel of your salvation." Paul states that it is the proclamation of the Word that sets forth the promises of God concerning salvation in His appointed redeemer. Paul continues, "in whom," that is, "in Christ" the anointed one who will bring full salvation by His work of redemption alone. This must include full atonement for sin and eternal salvation. Notice how the substance is Christ and not our faith, that this salvation is in Christ "in whom also, having believed," or we might say, having assented to, embraced, and rested in the gospel message that was preached about Jesus the Christ. Then he concludes with this assurance, that "you were sealed," here inferring that we have been restored legally to God with a promise of eternal restoration by the regenerating work of the Holy Spirit, a promise God cannot break, and that is why we were "sealed with the Holy Spirit of promise."

In this federal covenantal agreement, the Father and Son promised to send the Holy Spirit to regenerate, to apply Christ's salvation fully to those who are the elect. Paul says that this purpose is that the Holy Spirit "is the guarantee of our inheritance." God has given the Holy Spirit as the very means of assuring this eternal union with Him according to the eternal covenant of God's plan "until the redemption of the purchased possession." The purpose alone is that it has been decreed "to the praise of His glory." Paul explains God's purpose in the salvation of His chosen people (Christ's Church) was for the praise and honor of God! What is most notable in the text is that there is nothing ascribed as coming from man wherein he has contributed anything to this amazing salvation by grace alone. This is what Augustine believed about God's grace in soteriological thought, as Herman Bavinck states, "Augustine was the first to develop the doctrine of grace, taken not in the sense of a divine attribute, but in the sense of the benefits which God through Christ grants to the Church."

This development finds its expression in Pauline theology, as we have just shown. Philip Schaff asserts that Augustine maintains that every theological thought concerning salvific grace resides within the sovereignty of God, for Augustine maintains that God is the "Fountain of our imperial sovereignty."

This is Augustinianism, and its greater and fuller expression is found in the theology of that great French Reformer John Calvin.

Pelagius, however, rejected Augustine's concept of original sin (a doctrine that had been taught prior to Augustine by early Church Fathers also) and asserted that "free will" had not been affected by Adam's original sin in the Garden. Therefore, Adam's sin did not affect man's ability to do righteousness through his own initiative. He believed that if man was guilty of anything before God it was based on his own actual sins and not a result of the sin of Adam. In his "Letter to Demetrias," Pelagius wrote: "Over the years our sin gradually corrupts us, building an addiction and then holding us bound with what seems like the force of nature itself."

Pelagius thus rejected Augustine's doctrine of original sin, substitutionary atonement, and the necessity of justification by faith.

This doctrine of Pelagius was held to be in contradiction to the teaching of the Bible by both Augustine and Jerome, and violated well-known passages of Scripture, such as Romans 5:12–17 where the Apostle Paul wrote: "Therefore, just as through one man (Adam) sin (the transgression of God's Law) entered the world." This is a reference to the Garden of Eden when Adam and Eve both ate from the tree of knowledge of good and evil. The result was, "death (spiritual and physical) through sin, and thus death spread to all men." Adam's sin brought condemnation upon all people, all of Adam's posterity, the human race, "because all sinned." That is, all of the human race sinned in Adam's original sin.

Paul continues: "For until the law," the time when God gave to Moses the Law written in stone, he says that "sin was in the world." Here Paul asserts that sin was in all men prior to the law being given to Moses in stone. However, Paul says, "but sin is not imputed when there is no law." Thus, with the presence of law there is the presence of sin, the original sin of Adam. Paul writes in Romans 2:14–15 that the works of the Law—innate morality or the essence of the Ten Commandments—was already written on the constitutional nature of man. Therefore there is a law, and since there is a law, there is sin among men as a result of Adam's federal transgression. Adam had been given a commandment by special revelation—propositional truth—not to eat from the tree of the knowledge of good and evil. Adam disobeyed God's command and ate of the tree, thereby bringing condemnation upon himself and all mankind. Thus, Adam's sin reigned in all men even before the law was actually written on stone in the days of Moses. Paul continues: "Nevertheless death reigned from Adam to Moses, even over those who had not sinned according to the likeness of the transgression of Adam."

Note carefully that men did not have the same opportunity to choose to obey God like Adam did in the Garden. Nevertheless, Adam's sin of death reigned, meaning that it ruled all men as being condemned before God. Paul states that this first Adam "is a type of Him who was to come." Here we have the teaching of the first Adam in the Garden as being a type of the second and last Adam, that second Adam being Christ. The second Adam would do what the first Adam failed to do, obey God's Law or command. This obedience by the second Adam, Jesus Christ, is where He becomes our legal surety on behalf of the elect of the Father. Jesus Christ keeps the law of God on behalf of the elect. All men, even the elect, were born as sinners because of Adam's transgression. This original sin forensically or legally separated and condemned them from their birth, leaving them spiritually dead and physically dying from their first breath of air.

Paul goes on: "But the free gift is not like the offense." The gift of salvation is not like the first sin; it is just the opposite. Paul continues: "For if by the one man's offense many died, much more the grace of God and the gift by the grace of the one Man, Jesus Christ, abounded to many." In the first Adam all mankind died spiritually and physically because he failed to do what was commanded by God. However, with the second Adam we have this gift of grace given or abounding to the many (all the elect), and it brought those dead in sin back to life. How? It was based on Christ being the legal surety in salvation. In Christ's keeping the law perfectly, because He was without sin, His righteousness was accounted to the elect as a "foreign righteousness." Upon the basis of this righteousness of Christ, God declares (a legal declaration) that those who are "elect in Christ," when they exercise the faith that they are given by the Holy Spirit in regeneration, are legally restored to a right standing before God. Believers are sealed with the Holy Spirit as fulfilling the eternal promise of God in Christ to the elect of God. The apostle continues: "And the gift is not like that which came through the one who sinned. For the judgment which came from one offense resulted in condemnation, but the free gift which came from many offenses resulted in justification." Here, through the inspiration of the Holy Spirit, Paul has drawn out the meaning of the results of Adam's transgression over against Christ's atonement for sin. Christ's gift did not result in condemnation! Rather it resulted in salvation! Adam's sin resulted in judgment and thus condemnation. On the other hand, the free gift is "free" because a sinner can neither restore himself to nor place himself in a right standing with God. This is because man by nature is a violator of God's law from birth. This is what it means to be a sinner in Adam. Therefore, God must freely give salvation to man. It is called a "free gift" because it is of "grace," the unmerited favor of God. Christ's work of atonement results in our justification, that is, in God declaring us in Christ who is our salvation, right with Him. We are restored, forgiven of the original and our actual sins, and given eternal life based on the legal work of Christ at Calvary.

The apostle continues: "For if by the one man's offense death reigned through the one, much more those who receive abundance of grace and of the gift of righteousness will reign in life through the One, Jesus Christ." Here Paul rightfully concludes that death reigned through Adam in his one transgression in the Garden, and therefore sin reigned in all men bringing death, judgment, and condemnation before God. But for the elect of God, those who are always identified by believing the gospel, salvation is the abundance of grace. Salvation is the unmerited favor of God, not the works of man, or anything man might contribute to his salvation. It is a gift of righteousness. Why a gift? Because if man earns it, it is not a gift! It is just a payment for services rendered by man to God. But Paul says it is a gift of righteousness, wherein God has legally decreed the restoration of the elect with Himself at their appointed time in history. What is the decree? It is that we shall be ruled in life—that is in our salvation—by the one, Jesus Christ. This is the eternal security of the believer, and it is based on the eternal surety of Christ our salvation. This is why the elect cannot lose their salvation. Salvation's loss is impossible since believers contributed nothing to their legal standing with God. Christ's legal righteousness stands on our behalf, and He died once only for sin for all the elect, according to Hebrews 9:1–28.

St. Augustine, who was Bishop of Hippo, along with other theologians of the Church, held that Pelagius was guilty of denying the need for divine salvation as prior to the performance of good works. Let me state it this way. The Church believes that good works proceeded or a result from being justified, but they are not the cause for our justification.

Pelagius, however, maintained that the grace that was necessary for man to perform good and acceptable works to God, for the salvation of his soul, was found in the declaration of the law. Therefore man's sins needed to be forgiven on the basis of man's keeping the law of God, and this was done by meritorious effort through the absolute free will of man. According to Pelagius, man was perfectly able to fulfill the law apart from any divine aid of God's grace. Pelagius and his student Caelestius were charged with heresy, tried, and declared heretics by the Council of Carthage in 418. The Council condemned the doctrine of "free will," which asserted that a man can restore himself to a legal right standing with God based on his own meritorious works of righteousness. This condemned doctrine became known in the Church of Jesus Christ as the doctrine of Pelagianism.

Pelagianism eventually was partially reasserted in the Church and came to be more fully defined as a synthetic justification during the time of medieval Scholasticism. In this form it embraced human effort combined with God's grace. This is a synthesis of salvation by both God and man—a doctrine known as semi-pelagianism. Semi-pelagianism is fraught with the same heretical teaching as pelagianism since the essential principle is the unbridled free will of man to morally make the determination of whether he will or will not accept the gospel of Jesus Christ. Semi-pelagianism was condemned by the Council of Orange in 529.

What must be kept in mind is that the essential principles of this doctrine of "free will" persisted throughout the history of the church, only to reappear in medieval scholasticism. This doctrine is also found in renaissance humanism, Socinianism, and modern theological liberalism. I will not spend any more time with the doctrine in its "semi" developed form. What is important for us to realize is this: eventually God granted a reformation to the Church wherein the doctrine of salvation by grace alone, by Christ alone, through faith alone became the cornerstone of Protestant Christianity. This is the doctrine that was fundamental in breaking away from the Roman Catholic Church that had come to be dominated by the illegitimate ascendancy of the Papacy, along with its heretical, damnable doctrines of salvation based on the meritorious effort of man combined with the grace of God. However, we are not completely finished with this legalistic doctrine of salvation based on man's meritorious efforts.

In time, within Protestantism, there arose a new doctrinal formula that taught salvation was based on man's "free will," that is, man is free to choose salvation or reject it. In this new formula it was held that God's grace was withheld until the individual either accepted the gospel or rejected it. Only after man contributed his meritorious effort of "choosing"—a moral act of righteousness—would God then, and only then, justify him based on the work of Christ. This doctrine was known after its propagator Jacob Arminius (1560-1609 AD). Arminius was a professor in Holland and a member of the Dutch Reformed Church. This new doctrine became known as "Arminianism," named after Arminius its originator. It is clearly a step up from semi-pelagianism, and has been considered as "evangelical" simply because it claims that the grace to be granted after the exercise of the "free will of man" is based on the grace of God alone, in Christ alone, by faith alone. The problem is two-fold from the reformed and/or evangelical church perspective that believes in a salvation that precedes the exercise of faith as an act of man's will to believe.

First, the will of man is declared over and over again in Scripture as being in bondage to sin, and therefore man cannot morally choose to do what is right before God in order for God to show favor to him. The idea that man "morally wills to choose God," thereby granting the Holy Spirit to then regenerate the individual, is contrary to the clear teaching of Scripture. St. Paul declares in Romans 3:9–20 that all men are unrighteous, self-seeking, and cannot do any good as it relates to righteousness and salvation:

> What then? Are we better than they? Not at all. For we have previously charged both Jews and Greeks that they are all under sin. As it is written: "There is none righteous, no, not one; There is none who understands; There is none who seeks after God. They have all turned aside; They have together become unprofitable; There is none who does good, no, not one." "Their throat is an open tomb; With their tongues they have practiced deceit"; "The poison of asps is under their lips"; "Whose mouth is full of cursing and bitterness." "Their feet are swift to shed blood; Destruction and misery are in their ways; And the way of peace they have not known." "There is no fear of God before their eyes." Now we know that whatever the law says, it says to those who are under the law, that every mouth

may be stopped, and all the world may become guilty before God. Therefore by the deeds of the law no flesh will be justified in His sight, for by the law is the knowledge of sin.

The second problem deals with the premise that a sinful man can morally will himself to choose righteousness. The question might be asked in this way: "How does a sinful man who is morally bound in sin because of Adam's original sin, and his actual sins, morally choose to do righteousness when he is condemned as being morally sinful?" There has never been a biblical solution that has adequately answered this question. That is not to say that there have not been attempts to answer this question. Aminianism is such an attempt, but a poor one at best! Further, this act of the will includes the idea that faith is the precondition of salvation to be acted upon by man before God will infuse the Holy Spirit in regeneration. In other words, man must first believe or have faith in the promise of God as presented in the gospel message prior to regeneration by the Holy Spirit. Therefore, the emphasis is on faith and free will. In this doctrinal formula, faith is that meritorious act or effort of man wherein God is willing to respond by granting to him salvation by sending the Holy Spirit to regenerate the individual by applying Christ's atonement.

The problem however seems to have gotten worse. The Arminian has gotten himself into a deeper predicament. In this soteriological scenario, we now have "faith" as the substance of salvation that places the initial effort upon man's work of righteousness in morally willing himself to God. Salvation in this traditional teaching finds itself in the heritage of pelagianism! Man is saved by his own faith! Faith is not the gift of God, but the work of man! It is a work of the morally free will of man. Thus we see that pelagianism has once again gained a strong foothold in the Church of Jesus Christ, especially in the 20th and 21st century Church. This, as I see it, is the continuing plague of free-will moralism. This is a doctrine that we must be eternally vigilant in combating from generation to generation. It is a heresy that kills evangelical orthodox theology. Let's look closer at this doctrine.

Arminianism is in total contradiction to the doctrinal formula of salvation by grace alone. The grace of God is not alone in the Armianian scheme of salvation; rather, grace comes as a "gift" (actually as a payment) in Christ upon a moral action taken by man. It is asserting that man has in some way clearly "merited the favor of God" wherein God will grant grace because of his act of "faith," which he claims as man-made, not God-given. This clearly contradicts the clear teaching of Scripture. We clearly see this in Scripture. First, John writes in his gospel that: "But as many as received Him," that is, those who believed the gospel of Jesus Christ, "to them He gave the right to become children of God." Christ adopted them into the family of God, "to those who believe in His name," those who confessed the doctrine of Jesus Christ as the Son of God and Savior of men.

Now carefully note what brought about that adoption into the family of God. Paul says, "who were born," meaning regenerated by the Holy Spirit, which he says was "not of blood," that is to say, not by man's ability to atone through his own nor animal sacrifice (see Hebrews 9:11–15), "nor of the will of the flesh." Here John is pointing out that human effort, the actual works of man's hands, are insufficient to save any individual. Further, John says, "nor of the will of man." So it is not even by an act of man "willing to choose God," to make an act of "faith first." Rather John states, "but of God." It was God who granted those who believed to be birthed (born again) as children of God through Christ. It was the Holy Spirit who regenerated them prior to any act that they had done. No human actions, whether physical, mental, or spiritual are involved in regeneration. No works of the flesh or of the will of man will bring God's salvation upon any individual. Salvation is a gift and the gift cannot be merited by man physically, mentally, or spiritually, no matter what the intentions of a man may be! Thus faith cannot be a precondition for salvation. That means that faith does not precede the Holy Spirit in regeneration because St. Paul identifies "faith" as a gift from God and not an act or work of man. The declaration of this revelatory teaching is found in Ephesians 2:1–10, where the apostle states: "And you He made alive." It is God who makes the believer alive, who is dead in trespasses and sins. As an unbeliever we were not sick, but dead; we were being ruled by sin and could not do anything that would bring life by our own ability. Paul continues: "in which you once walked according to the course of this world, according to the prince of the power of the air, the spirit who now works in the sons of disobedience." Now Paul says that our actions in being ruled by death and condemnation made us work according to the "course of the world" and "according to the prince of the power of the air," who is Satan. The result is that the spirit of disobedience is now working in us as "sons of disobedience." No man in this condition has an ability to do righteousness by some pretended moral free will wherein he can, of his own ability, independently of God, believe the gospel of Christ. This is simply religious humanism; it is "free will moralism."

Man, says the apostle, is an enemy of God—unwilling to do what God commands of him. He states: "among whom also we all once conducted ourselves in the lusts of our flesh, fulfilling the desires of the flesh and of the mind." We, says Paul, conducted our lives in the lusts of our flesh; we willingly fulfilled the desires of the flesh and not the will of God! These desires were not limited to the flesh, but were also desires of the mind of man. If these were our desires of the flesh and mind of man; and if these were the things we chose in the course of this world, and in this way being ruled by Satan—how can a man suddenly break that ruling of the will of the flesh and mind and become a morally good individual seeking the favor of God? The apostle proclaims that the opposite is true. Men are willingly doing the work as "sons of disobedience" because of the spirit that is at work in them! Paul concludes by stating: "and were by nature children of wrath, just as the others." Here is Paul's answer: we could not have done such a thing as freely willing ourselves unto a saving faith in Jesus Christ. We are our own very "nature," that includes the whole man, sinners. That is, we were the "children of wrath," the sons of disobedience. In this condition or state, it is not God whom we wanted to serve, rather it was Satan. How can an unclean thing become clean when its very nature is unclean? The Prophet Jeremiah wrote in 13:23: "Can the Ethiopian change his skin or the leopard its spots? Then may you also do good who are accustomed to do evil?" No man can contribute to his salvation. Paul himself states: "But God, who is rich in mercy, because of His great love with which He loved us, even when we were dead in trespasses, made us alive together with Christ (by grace you have been saved)." Paul clearly declares that it is God's great mercy, His love, that even when we were "dead" in our sins, it was God who made us "alive" in the work of Christ. We could not contribute one thing that would bring us before the judgment seat of God and demonstrate why He owed us salvation, or that we even deserved salvation. All we could bring to Him of our righteousness He considered as "filthy rags." The Prophet Isaiah wrote: "But we are like an unclean thing. And all our righteousness is like filthy rags" (Isaiah 64:6).

It is by grace that we are saved—by the unmerited favor of God. Thus Paul states that God has therefore, "raised us up together, and made us sit together in the heavenly places in Christ Jesus." We are "positionally" saved in Christ, who now is ruling and reigning over all things, but especially the things regarding the salvation of His church, so "that in the ages to come He might show the exceeding riches of His grace in His kindness toward us in Christ Jesus." God's promise will eventually be realized in the resurrection. It is then that we shall share with our resurrected Savior eternal life in the New Heavens and New Earth. Continuing, Paul then declares: "For by grace you have been saved through faith, and that not of yourselves; it is the gift of God, not of works, lest anyone should boast." Christ is the substance of salvation, and our salvation comes by the "instrument" of faith. That "faith" is only an instrument by which we are enabled to believe the gospel of Jesus Christ. It is not a work or act made by man. It is God's gift in order that we who are dead in sin might be able to become alive and believe the gospel of Jesus Christ. This faith, says Paul, is "not of works." For if it was of man's own ability to believe, man could then boast that God had to save him because he produced the faith necessary to receive the grace of God for his salvation. Paul says, "lest anyone should boast." The "grace" of the Arminian faith is not very amazing at all, because what is amazing is man's faith! Therefore they should sing "Amazing Faith" because it is the only ground upon which God could save them. They will profess that "I once was hard of sight, but by my own ability I can now see, and now God must shed His grace on me!" In the tenth verse, St. Paul really explains the sovereign free grace of God in salvation! He states: "For we (elect believers) are His (God's) workmanship, created (renewed and transformed) in Christ Jesus for good works." Yes, good works are a part of the doctrine of salvation. However, they are not the cause of God's grace. Rather they are the result of His sovereign free grace. By God's free grace we can produce good works that are acceptable to God. Paul goes on to assert that these good works are a part of the salvation "which God prepared beforehand that we should walk in them." God ordained that the elect would walk according to the saving will of God, and that redeeming grace will produce good works in us, and therefore be manifested before all men that we have a living faith.

Conclusion

The first and most lethal form of legalism that should be identified in Christian theology is that form of doctrine that in anyway detracts from the absolute total work of salvation by grace alone, in Christ alone, by faith alone. It is God who alone makes men alive in Christ, and grants them faith and repentance as a result of His regenerating them by the Holy Spirit. Whether it is Pelagianism, semi-pelagianism, or Arminanism, any doctrine that allows for any meritorious effort by man in the work of salvation is legalism! This legalism is the plague of free-will moralism, and the modern church is polluted with this heretical doctrine. If we do not recognize the first most rudimentary form of legalism in theology, it is doubtful that we will be able to root out any other variations that we find in sanctification or ecclesiastical practices. Purity of doctrine, biblical orthodoxy, is the only means to developing an orthopraxis individually and corporately that will be pleasing and honoring to God. We are called to confront and refute this pelagian doctrine of free-will moralism in order that the Church might correctly align all of its teachings with God's sovereign free grace in Christ. Then, and only then, will we be free of this heresy. It is the truth of the God's Word alone that sets the Christian free so that he shall be free indeed.

Judging vs. Biblical Discernment

John MacArthur

Receive my words
And treasure my commandments within you,
Make your ear attentive to wisdom,
Incline your heart to understanding;
For if you cry for discernment,
Lift your voice for understanding;
If you seek her as silver
And search for her as for hidden treasures;
Then you will discern the fear of the LORD
And discover the knowledge of God.
For the LORD gives wisdom;
From His mouth come knowledge and understanding.
Proverbs 2:1–6 (NASB)

One of the most commonly-quoted but frequently misconstrued verses in all of Scripture is Matthew 7:1, popularly paraphrased as "Judge not, lest you be judged." Even the most biblically illiterate unbeliever knows those words. People love to wield that phrase as a kind of all–purpose retort to any hint of biblical reproof or correction. The typical skeptic may be seething with contempt for the Bible, utterly ignorant of everything else Jesus ever said, and totally enslaved to the world, the flesh, and the devil. But he will invariably quote *that* verse with all the gravitas of a seasoned seminary lecturer, using a tone of devout finality that suggests God has spoken on this matter and any further discussion would be the ultimate sacrilege.

Thus the skeptic dismisses even godly counsel with a face-slap from a proof-text that has been twisted and wrenched out of its context. Ironic, isn't it? Those who mishandle God's Word in that way are guilty of precisely the kind of hypocrisy Jesus goes on to condemn in the verses immediately following His "judge not" admonition (vv. 2–6).

Of course, biblical texts are always best understood in light of their immediate context, and Matthew 7:1 is no exception. In verse 2 Jesus Himself explains His actual point: "In the way you judge, you will be judged; and by your standard of measure, it will be measured to you." He is not prohibiting sound, righteous judgment. He is warning (and rebuking) smug, self-appointed, self-righteous spiritual leaders who held people to a more burdensome standard than they themselves could possibly bear (Matthew 23:4). It was a man-made, legalistic standard of their own making, too (Mark 7:9–13). Their judgments were therefore tainted, wicked, hypocritical, oppressive—full of unwarranted pride in themselves and undue scorn for others.

But Jesus clearly desires for us to make sound judgments about important matters, because elsewhere He urges us to judge righteously. He makes this vital distinction in John 7:24: "Do not judge according to appearance, but *judge with righteous judgment*" (emphasis added). Notice, the last phrase in that verse is an imperative; it is a command that we are obligated to obey. Christ holds us responsible to apply justice and holy wisdom; making necessary judgments in a careful, impartial, and discerning way; tempering judgment with mercy, as God Himself does (James 2:12–13).

It should be obvious, then, that Matthew 7:1 cannot mean we are forbidden to make any kind of judgment whatsoever. If that were the case, Jesus' teaching elsewhere—starting with the remainder of the Sermon on the Mount—would make no sense at all. In the culminating illustration of this very sermon Jesus calls for a judgment to be made. He makes a sharp contrast between the small gateway to a narrow road that leads to life, and the wide on-ramp to a broad thoroughfare that leads to destruction. Jesus is urging His hearers to evaluate the two ways, distinguish between them, and choose accordingly.

He then concludes the sermon with that famous illustration of two men—one who was wise and built his house on solid rock, the other who was foolish and built on sand. As He wraps up His sermon with that contrast, Jesus admonishes His hearers to listen carefully to His words and act on His teaching (vv. 24, 26).

The implication is impossible to miss. We have a duty to discern between the right gate and the wrong one, to follow the true path instead of the much-traveled thoroughfare, and to build on a solid foundation rather than on weak and shifting sand. Note, too, that Jesus was speaking of spiritual realities, not things that can be marked on a physical map. His teaching demands that we make judgments about spiritual things, and that we judge correctly—by exercising careful, precise, biblical discernment.

This truth is not limited to the Sermon on the Mount, of course. Throughout Scripture it is abundantly clear that we *do* need to judge properly between truth and falsehood, spiritual virtues and fleshly lusts, earthly wisdom and biblical truth, sound doctrine and demonic lies, true righteousness and mere hypocrisy. The Bereans were *commended* for judging even the teaching of the apostles by comparing it to the biblical standard (Acts 17:11). As a matter of fact, one of the most important signs of spiritual maturity is an ability to make precisely that kind of judgment. A person cannot properly digest biblical truth at all without learning to differentiate properly between sound and unsound doctrine. "Solid food is for the mature, who because of practice have their senses trained to discern good and evil" (Hebrews 5:14). In short, those who suggest that it's always wrong to make any kind of judgment are themselves guilty of making a false judgment.

What Is Discernment?

The Greek verb translated "discern" in the New Testament is *diakrino,* meaning, literally, "to separate; to make a distinction." Peter uses the word with a negative modifier in Acts 15:9 to answer the Judaizers' error, citing the conversion of Cornelius's household as proof that God "made no distinction" between Jews and Gentiles.

So the biblical word for discernment speaks of the ability to make keen and careful distinctions. A discerning person is someone who can discriminate accurately between truth and error. Discernment starts with the recognition that righteousness and lawlessness cannot be made partners; light and darkness have no fellowship; there is no harmony between Christ and Belial; believers and unbelievers have nothing in common; and the temple of God has no agreement with idols (2 Corinthians 6:14–16). Scripture gives us those contrasts in stark black and white. It is sheer folly to pretend that every moral judgment must be shaded in tones of gray. If the goal of discernment is to separate truth from error, it is both foolish and spiritually deadly to blend everything together in the mud of endless relativism.

But could anything be more at odds with the spirit of the present age? The prevailing opinion today is that stark clarity is not only impossible; it is undesirable as well. Mystery is celebrated; certainty is scorned. Questions are encouraged; answers are repudiated. Truth itself is viewed as an outdated concept. Blurry lines, shades of gray, compromise, ambiguity, and equivocation are the preferred tools of human discourse. Nothing is deemed absolute except the absence of any absolute standard. Certainty and assurance are condemned as arrogance.

And confidence in the revealed truth of Scripture is the most politically incorrect certainty of all.

The church, desperate to catch up with the times, seems to have lost the will to discriminate between truth and error. Many professing Christians today are just as committed to ideological relativism as their unbelieving neighbors. Brian McLaren, for example, whose books are published by Christian publishers and promoted in Christian bookstores, says it upsets him to hear any pastor proclaim biblical truth with conviction. "The more sure he seems, the less I find myself wanting to be a Christian," he writes. "Life isn't that simple, answers aren't that clear, and nothing is that sure."[1]

With the decline of biblical conviction, the evangelical movement has been overrun with storytellers, entertainers, entrepreneurs, mystics, and self-proclaimed prophets. They operate on the basis of personal feelings and individual experience while heedlessly (and sometimes deliberately) trampling the authority of Scripture. Some influential church leaders openly discount the importance of sound doctrine. They practice a "teach anything, criticize nothing" policy, effectively spurning discernment altogether.

The head of the world's largest charismatic television network, for example, is blithely apathetic about the need for careful doctrinal discernment. In his words, "one theologian's

---

1. Brian McLaren, *A New Kind of Christian* (San Francisco: Jossey–Bass, 2003), 14.

heresy is another theologian's orthodoxy."[2] His network features a nightly lineup of gospel-twisters, hucksters, heretics, and prosperity-gospel charlatans. He claims that his stable of faith-healers and televangelists would all affirm the basics of the Apostles' Creed, and, based on that minimalist profession of faith, he believes it would be wrong and uncharitable for anyone to subject them to any further sort of doctrinal appraisal. "The true apologist [would] NEVER judg[e] a brother or sister by name with whom he may disagree," he writes.[3] To do so, he claims, is hurtful to the cause of Christ. He opts instead for the don't-worry-be-happy approach to doctrine: "When we get [to heaven] the true believers should have worked it out in agape love and, if not, the Lord Himself will reveal to all who was right and who was wrong."[4]

That attitude is now surprisingly widespread among people who self-identify as evangelicals, and it has been devastating to the cause of truth among our congregations. An undiscerning church has no defense against false teaching.

It is quite true, of course, that exercising real discernment and being merely judgmental are two vastly different things. There are people who seem to take sinful delight in fault-finding, and they do sometimes try to justify their censorious spirit in the name of biblical discernment. But it isn't terribly hard to distinguish true discernment from mere judgmental-ism. Watch out for the full-time critic who constantly reproves and rebukes others, but rarely offers any edifying instruction or

---

2. Paul Crouch, in the foreword to James R. Spencer, *Heresy Hunters* (Lafayette, LA: Huntington House, 1993), vii.

3. *Ibid.*, viii.

4. *Ibid.*, ix.

exhortation when he is the one doing the teaching. Beware the self-styled discernment expert who is *always* hostile, scornful, or angry toward the subjects of his criticism. There is a place for indignation, sternness, and even sanctified sarcasm, but animosity should not be anyone's default mode. Also, be especially cautious when you encounter someone who seems to take delight in uncovering others' sins or constantly publishing shocking exposés. Gossip, guilt by association, mud-slinging, and personal slurs are fleshly weapons. "The anger of man does not achieve the righteousness of God" (James 1:20). Some who fancy themselves skilled in the art of discernment are merely being fleshly and factious.

But in these postmodern times, the far greater danger comes from the opposite end of the spectrum. Evangelical churches are full of people who simply "will not endure sound doctrine; but wanting to have their ears tickled, they [have accumulated] for themselves teachers in accordance to their own desires, and [have turned] away their ears from the truth and [turned] aside to myths" (2 Timothy 4:3–4). It is tragic that real discernment is considered out of fashion by so many evangelicals, because the church has never been more desperately in need of sober, discerning hearts and distinct, authoritative voices to call the people of God back to the clarity and authority of His Word.

The Apostle Paul outlines a very simple three-part strategy for discernment in 1 Thessalonians 5:21–22: "Examine everything carefully; hold fast to that which is good; abstain from every form of evil." Each imperative in that triad is vital.

Examine Everything Carefully

Paul is writing to the church at Thessalonica. The Thessalonian believers had not been as careful as the Bereans to examine what they were taught (Acts 17:11). Both of Paul's epistles to them reveal how susceptible they were to confusion from false teaching. Someone had evidently planted among them the fear that believers who died before the return of Christ would miss the Second Coming completely, and Paul had to correct that misunderstanding (1 Thessalonians 4:13–18). Whoever was sowing confusion among them then forged a letter as if from Paul, suggesting that they had already missed the coming of the Lord after all (2 Thessalonians 2:1–2). That's one of the main reasons Paul wrote a second epistle; he had to reassure them once again and reiterate precisely what he had taught before. ("Do you not remember that while I was still with you, I was telling you these things?" v. 5.)

So as Paul draws his first letter to this church to a close, he turns to the issue of discernment. The whole epistle has been an expression of pastoral love and encouragement. He has admonished the Thessalonians, commended them, reassured them, exhorted them, and reminded them that the Lord is coming. Now he sums up his charge to the church in verse 6: "Be alert and sober." Then he concludes the epistle with a list of simple, basic commands that explain in detail what it means to be "alert and sober"—people "of the day" as opposed to drunken revelers at night (vv. 7–8).

Specifically, in order to maintain vigilance and stay ready for the Lord's return, they needed to encourage and edify one another (v. 11); appreciate the labors of their ministers (v. 12); esteem their leaders highly (v. 13); live in peace with one another (v. 13); "admonish the unruly, encourage the faint-hearted, help the weak, be patient with everyone" (v. 14); and don't repay evil with evil, but seek after good (v.15).

Then comes that familiar string of compact commands—five of the shortest verses in the New Testament: "Rejoice always; pray without ceasing; in everything give thanks; for this is God's will for you in Christ Jesus. Do not quench the Spirit; do not despise prophetic utterances" (vv. 16–20).

The next words are the first of three imperatives dealing specifically with the subject of discernment: "Examine everything *carefully*" (v. 21). The italics signify that the word "carefully" was added in the translation. The King James Version says, "prove all things," and the English Standard Version simply says, "test everything." The addition of *"carefully"* in the New American Standard Bible is a good one, however, because it conveys the true sense of the Greek word *dokimazo* ("examine"). That word was commonly used to signify the meticulous process of assaying precious metals. It suggests the idea of putting something into a crucible and subjecting it to extreme heat or acid. If it's impure gold, the dross will be burned away. If it's not gold at all, the fire will reveal that, too (*cf.* 1 Corinthians 3:13). So the word "examine" speaks of giving something the closest possible scrutiny for the purpose of determining whether it is true or counterfeit.

Remember, this admonition comes at the end of the epistle as the culminating charge in a list of basic duties. It is a reminder that discernment is as vital to healthy Christian devotion as prayer, rejoicing, and thanksgiving.

Furthermore, this command is addressed to the rank-and-file people of the church—not the leadership only. Many Christians tend to think of discernment as a uniquely pastoral duty. It is, indeed, a vital qualification for every man in ministry (Titus 1:9). Elders in the church are responsible not only to feed and lead the flock of God, but also to protect the sheep from wolves—false teachers who corrupt and deny truth and destroy souls in the process. Defending the fold from such intruders calls for skill in discernment. This is such an essential part of the shepherds' task that those who lack the will to do it should not be in ministry at all.

But pastors and elders have no monopoly on discernment. Paul is cataloguing basic Christian responsibilities. This short bullet list of duties applies to each one of us. Every Christian needs to cultivate discernment.

The command is tied by a conjunction ("but") to the verse that immediately precedes it. What, specifically, were they to examine so carefully? "Prophetic utterances" (v. 20). Paul was urging them to test *everything they were taught*—no matter who the teacher was (*cf.* Galatians 1:8–9)—by comparing the teaching with Scripture, using the same careful strategy the Bereans employed.

Incidentally, the phrase "prophetic utterances" is not a reference to every aspiring prophet's attempts at soothsaying. Paul is talking about the authoritative apostolic message. He was not envisioning some chaotic charismatic outpouring of weird private prophecies, as if it were our duty to heed every deluded clairvoyant and try to sort out truth from an admixture of false claims and human fantasies. False prophecies and failed prognostications *should* be despised (Deuteronomy 18:20–22).

But Paul was talking about true, authoritative prophetic utterances such as the Thessalonians had heard directly from him. They did not have the complete New Testament in written form yet, of course. All the gospel teaching they heard at first came to them from Paul with full apostolic authority. It was the same teaching that is now preserved for us in the New Testament. It was, in truth, the authoritative and effectual Word of God (1 Thessalonians 2:13). Paul had already commended them for receiving that message with genuine saving faith, but here he also urges the Thessalonians to be like their noble neighbors, the Bereans. They needed to learn to subject every teaching they heard to careful scrutiny under the infallible light of Scripture (Acts 17:11). Paul wanted them to examine thoroughly every doctrine they were taught, whether the preacher was Paul (who according to Galatians 1:11 received the gospel by direct revelation) or Timothy, who taught from Paul's epistles (and other Scriptures) and who spearheaded the process of training subsequent generations of church leaders to teach likewise from the written Word (1 Timothy 4:11; 2 Timothy 2:2).

In other words, whenever the true Word of God is faithfully proclaimed, that is a "prophetic utterance" in the sense Paul means here. This meaning of the word *prophecy* is stressed in 1 Corinthians 14:3–4, where Paul writes: "One who prophesies speaks to men for edification and exhortation and consolation. [He] edifies the church." Any biblical sermon, prepared and delivered correctly with appropriate conviction, is a true prophetic utterance according to the way Paul employs the expression.

So this is a command to subject every truth-claim to the test of Scripture. Again, that is the duty of every Christian. We're not to believe everything we hear just because the preacher says he comes in the name of Christ (2 John 7–11). We are not to be like "children, tossed here and there by waves, and carried about by every wind of doctrine, by the trickery of men, by craftiness in deceitful scheming" (Ephesians 4:14). Gullibility is not a virtue. Searching the Scriptures to see whether something is true is not uncharitable. Scripture says that is the *noble* thing to do.

Hold Fast to Whatever Is Good

The kind of discernment Paul is encouraging the Thessalonians to cultivate is the polar opposite of a merely academic approach to truth and sound doctrine. A merely clinical examination followed by a neutral analysis is not what

Paul has in mind. Authentic discernment calls for a thoughtful, cautious, but *active* twofold response.

First of all, he urges a positive response to whatever is good: "Hold fast to that which is good" (v. 21). He says the same thing in Romans 12:9: "Abhor what is evil; cling to what is good." He wants all believers to own the truth, hold tightly to it, and treat it as a treasure to be safeguarded. Paul himself had that perspective of truth. It was a stewardship he had been entrusted with (1 Corinthians 9:17), and as Timothy's mentor he labored to instill the same attitude in him: "O Timothy, guard what has been entrusted to you" (1 Timothy 6:20). "Retain the standard of sound words which you have heard from me . . . Guard, through the Holy Spirit who dwells in us, the treasure which has been entrusted to you" (2 Timothy 1: 13–14).

There is a definite note of militancy in Paul's frequent appeals to hold fast, cling to, and guard the deposit of truth. The person who turns his back or abandons the truth when it is under attack is not a faithful steward. Nor is this a call to hold the truth privately, keeping it to ourselves. Our duty is to proclaim it, defend it when necessary, and answer every challenge against it. There is no place in this command for appeasement, compromise, or indifference in the face of threats to the truth. Indeed those are the very tendencies Paul is hoping to eliminate in Thessalonica.

But the thrust of this imperative is wholly and enthusiastically positive. The verb translated "hold fast" carries the connotation of a tight embrace—not a casual assent or a nod of agreement, but a whole-hearted, passionate commitment to the truth.

Love for the truth is one of the necessary features of true saving faith. In 2 Thessalonians 2:10, Paul describes un-believers as "those who perish, because they did not receive the love of the truth so as to be saved." Thus Scripture treats love for the truth as one of the distinguishing features of authentic saving faith. Any brand of "faith" that is devoid of such love is no faith at all.

Similarly, in 1 Corinthians 15:2, Paul says the proof of authentic faith is that it holds fast the truth of the gospel. "You are saved, *if* you hold fast the word which I preached to you." Conversely, Paul says those who abandon the truth have "believed in vain." He's not suggesting that regenerate people can lose their salvation; he is saying that a failure to persevere in the truth is proof that the apostate's belief was empty and superficial to begin with; it was never saving faith at all. That is precisely what the Apostle John said about apostates: "They went out from us, but they were not really of us; for if they had been of us, they would have remained with us; but they went out, in order that it might be shown that they all are not of us" (1 John 2:19).

Paul was not questioning the salvation of the Thessalonians, however. He made clear from the outset of this epistle that he was confident in their election (1:4). He commended them repeatedly for the way they received the gospel from the very start: "Our gospel did not come to you in word only, but also in power and in the Holy Spirit and with full conviction" (v. 5). "You became an example to all the believers in Macedonia and in Achaia. For the word of the Lord has sounded forth from you, not only in Macedonia and Achaia, but also in every place your faith toward God has gone forth, so that we have no need to say anything" (vv. 7–8). "You turned to God from idols to serve a living and true God" (v. 9). The epistle is full of confident statements about the Thessalonians' faith: "When you received the word of God which you heard from us, you accepted it not as the word of men, but for what it really is, the word of God, which also performs its work in you who believe" (2:13).

But while He was confident that the Thessalonians' faith was generally sound and genuine, he saw that they were weaker than they should have been in the discipline of discernment. Paul wanted them to cultivate their love for truth and develop a Berean-style commitment to distinguishing the truth from error.

Paul would have had no sympathy whatsoever for the postmodern notion that the way to achieve true unity is to lay doctrine aside and cultivate good works and personal relationships instead. This is a relentless refrain in the rhetoric of so-called Emergence religion: Christians should worry less about being right and more about being and doing good.[5] The Apostle Paul said good deeds and purity of doctrine are *both* vital (Titus 2:7), but sound doctrine is foundational. Good works are the natural fruit and the adornment that make the doctrine of God attractive (vv. 1, 10).

That is not to say that the truth will always be attractive to unbelievers. Fallen people love darkness rather than light, because their deeds are evil (John 3:19). The gospel is a stumbling block to Jews and foolishness to Greeks (1 Corinthians 1:23). The cross is an offense to the whole world (Romans 9:33). It is not our prerogative to tone down the truth, soften it, or alter it in any way for the sake of eliminating the offense. Indeed, to do that is the opposite of what Paul means when he says "hold fast."

Notice, no teaching is exempt from Paul's command to "examine everything carefully." If it was noble for the Bereans to put the apostolic message under the light of Scripture in

---

5. See, for example, McLaren, 61.

order to verify the teaching, then no teacher, no preacher, no doctor of divinity—and certainly no modern prophet—has any right to claim immunity from critical examination. "Examine *everything* carefully." Paul has elevated the importance of discernment above any scholastic honor, any ecclesiastical office, or any revelatory gift.

This much ought to be clear: nothing that is not in full agreement with the Word of God can possibly qualify as "that which is good." The Greek word translated "good" speaks of value and virtue—good character, not merely beauty or usefulness. The word speaks of something that is really and authoritatively true, not merely something that looks good superficially. There's a stark and deliberate contrast between "that which is good" in 1 Thessalonians 5:21 and "every form of evil" in verse 22. It is the difference between the truth and a lie; sound doctrine versus false teaching; light and darkness; righteousness and evil. Nothing could be further from Paul's meaning here than the popular pragmatic notion that "good" is any idea or tactic that's useful for drawing a crowd, entertaining people, or gaining the appreciation of the unchurched masses.

God's Word is what defines *good*. Indeed, Scripture is the distilled essence of what Paul means by "that which is good." Whatever accords with Scripture is therefore to be treasured, guarded, and held fast.

But that's only part of the work of discernment. That is merely the positive side of the equation.

Shun Every Form of Evil

The negative aspect of discernment is succinctly expressed in 1 Thessalonians 5:22: "Abstain from every form of evil." Paul employs an emphatic Greek verb, *apecho*—"shun," or "keep your distance." The expression has connotations of abhorrence, loathing, and revulsion. It is the proper response to anything impure or morally filthy. It is the very same word Paul used a few verses previously when he wrote: "Abstain from sexual immorality" (1 Thessalonians 4:3). Peter used the same word in a similar context: "Abstain from fleshly lusts" (1 Peter 2:11).

Bear in mind the context here at the end of 1 Thessalonians. Paul is talking about our response to people who claim to speak for God ("prophetic utterances," v. 20). He says to examine carefully everything they say, and shun "every form of evil." So the context suggests this applies particularly to false doctrine. The principle clearly applies, of course, to evil behavior, evil companionship, and "every [other] form of evil." But Paul is specifically addressing the problem of false doctrine—teachers who claim to be speaking prophetically when in fact they are spreading error and false doctrine. Examine their teaching carefully, critically, Paul says, and if it doesn't agree with Scripture, shun it.

That puts false teaching in its proper light. It is a gross evil that must be shunned in exactly the same manner we would recoil from sexual immorality and fleshly lusts. False teaching is no better than the grossest of moral evils; it is arguably worse. The comparative gravity of false teaching is seen in the fact that Jesus was known as a friend of publicans and sinners (Luke 7:34), but he was an outspoken and relentless adversary of Pharisaical legalism.

Incidentally, when Paul says, "examine everything carefully," he is not ordering us to become full-time students of error and evil. Some people who fancy themselves apologists and discernment experts immerse themselves in studying cults and human philosophies more than they study Scripture. It quickly becomes a dangerous obsession. That's not what Paul is calling for here. Remember, the *truth* is what we should cling to. Evil is what we must shun. To the church at Rome Paul wrote: "Do not be overcome by evil, but overcome evil with good" (Romans 12:21). And, "I want you to be wise in what is good, and innocent in what is evil" (16:19).

Many people are familiar with 1 Thessalonians 5:22 from the King James translation: "Abstain from all appearance of evil." That version is often quoted and sometimes misapplied as if Paul's chief concern had to do with the appearance of things—as if he were mandating abstinence from anything that looks bad. I once spoke with a man who insisted no Christian should ever ride a motorcycle. It has the appearance of something evil, he said, because motorcycles are associated with biker gangs.

That isn't really the point of this text. The Greek word translated "appearance" is *eidos*, which is translated "form" in Luke 3:22 ("the Holy Spirit descended upon Him in bodily form like a dove") and John 5:37 ("You have neither heard His voice at any time nor seen His form"). Paul's point is not that everything that appears evil must be avoided on the basis of what it looks like. He is saying rather that whatever *is* evil in character must be shunned no matter what form it takes—even when the false teacher comes disguised as an angel of light, claiming to want peace and unity.

One other common misunderstanding of this text needs to be corrected. When Paul says, "Hold fast to that which is good; abstain from every form of evil," he is not urging the Thessalonians to try a little bit of everything, eat the meat, and spit out the bones. I've heard people use that expression in a way that seems to dismiss or minimize the grave danger of heresy and alternative gospels. Paul wants the church to turn away completely from false prophets and purveyors of different gospels—repudiate them altogether. He is not suggesting that we should look for nuggets of truth in the doctrines taught by false teachers. He gives no latitude whatsoever for blending bits of gospel with popular ideas borrowed from other religions, cultural fads, highbrow philosophies, lowbrow entertainment, secular psychology, or whatever is currently popular in the world.

We're warned frequently in Scripture about the subtlety of Satan. He disguises himself as an angel of light. He quotes Scripture. He makes arguments that sound reasonable. But his specialty is twisting the truth, mixing it with lies, and giving evil the appearance of good. That is why we must examine everything with the utmost care, embracing teaching that concurs with Scripture and shunning everything else.

How vital is discernment? It is the difference between infantile gullibility and mature faith (Hebrews 5:13–14). It is the mark of authentic, vibrant, abundant love for Christ (Philippians 1:9). And it is the ultimate difference between someone who functions in the flesh and a truly spiritual person: "A natural man does not accept the things of the Spirit of God, for they are foolishness to him; and he cannot understand them, because they are spiritually appraised. But he who is spiritual appraises all things, yet he himself is appraised by no one" (1 Corinthians 2:14–15).

Stand Fast in Liberty
Phil Johnson

"So, brothers, we are not children of the slave
but of the free woman" (Galatians 4:31 ESV).

Christian liberty is a major theme in the New Testament, starting with the earliest recorded event in Jesus' public teaching ministry. In His very first sermon in his hometown synagogue, Jesus unrolled the scroll to Isaiah 61:1 and read from that ancient prophecy to announce that He had come "to proclaim liberty to the captives . . . to set at liberty those who are oppressed" (Luke 4:18). He later told His disciples, "You will know the truth, and the truth will set you free" (John 8:32). Then He added, "If the Son sets you free, you will be free indeed" (v. 36).

The same theme looms large in the writings of the Apostle Paul. His teaching is full of references to our freedom in Christ. "Where the Spirit of the Lord is, there is freedom" (2 Corinthians 3:17). "The law of the Spirit of life has set you free in Christ Jesus" (Romans 8:2). "You were called to freedom, brothers" (Galatians 5:13). Furthermore, when Paul speaks of Christian liberty, his language is always categorical and unapologetic. He had been saved out of a rigorous system of religious bondage, and he reveled in the freedom Christ gave him.

Many Christians seem confused by the idea of Christian liberty—even a bit fearful of it. What does it mean to be set free spiritually, and what are the limits of Christian liberty? How do we sort out the various disagreements among Christians regarding questionable activities? What is our duty with regard to the styles and standards of secular culture? Questions like those are pervasive in every community of believers.

The very idea of *liberty* is at odds with what some people think the Christian life is all about. Their concept of holiness is dominated by a list of taboos and restrictions. They talk as if the word *righteousness* was synonymous with strict rules about what Christians are *not* free to do. They tend to cringe and get defensive when the subject of Christian liberty comes up.

That way of thinking is fleshly, not spiritual. It mirrors the spirit of first-century Pharisaism. The Pharisees were obsessed with rules governing public behavior mainly because "they loved the glory that comes from man more than the glory that comes from God" (John 12:43). Their religion therefore consisted mostly of doing things to be seen by other people (Matthew 6:5; 23:5). Jesus dismissed the whole system as a form of cruel and carnal bondage (Luke 11:46).

In stark contrast, Scripture defines the Christian life as a life of complete and total liberty. In Galatians 5:1, Paul gives this strong, unequivocal command: "For freedom Christ has set us free; stand firm therefore, and do not submit again to a yoke of slavery." The apostle clearly regarded freedom in Christ as a sacred trust to be carefully guarded. Liberty is not just one optional benefit of our salvation, but it lies at the very heart of God's saving purpose. *"For freedom* Christ has set us free."

That verse perfectly sums up Paul's answer to the legalism that had infected the Galatian churches. It is not a complex lesson about some abstract doctrine. It is a simple, practical prescription. It is not merely a suggestion, but an emphatic command: *stand firm in your liberty*.

There is a pressing tone of urgency in the exhortation. No wonder. A major doctrinal crisis was brewing in the Galatian churches. The believers in that region were mainly Gentiles with pagan backgrounds whose biblical knowledge was sparse. But they had believed the gospel in response to Paul's preaching. Then, apparently, when Paul's ministry took him elsewhere, a group of false teachers came to Galatia and told the Galatians that they could not be truly and fully saved unless they were circumcised (cf. Acts 15:1). In other words, they insisted that Gentiles could not fully enter into the Christian community unless they first became proselytes to Judaism.

That, of course, would make Old Testament ceremonial law a prerequisite to conversion, thus nullifying the principle of justification by faith. In effect, these Judaizing false teachers were trying to make Christianity a legalistic religion of works, just like Pharisaism. In fact, according to Acts 15:5, they "belonged to the party of the Pharisees." They professed faith in Christ, but they were altering the gospel with an erroneous application of Old Testament law. They were such determined foes of spiritual liberty that they could not bear the principle of *sola gratia* (grace alone), so they replaced the true gospel with a modified, super-ficially Christianized version of the old Pharisaical works system. In Galatians 1:8–9, the Apostle Paul anathematizes them, em-ploying some of the strongest condemnatory language you will find in any of his epistles.

The words of Galatians 5:1 are likewise infused with passion as Paul *commands* the Galatians to stand firm in the liberty with which Christ has set them free. He uses the Greek word *steko,* "be stationary; persevere." It's the same term used in 1 Corinthians 16:13: "Be watchful, *stand firm in the faith,* act like men, be strong." He is calling for guardedness with a militant posture. We're to lay hold of liberty and refuse to let go of it. This is a holy obligation—to fix ourselves in defense of Christian liberty.

What does that liberty entail and how far does it extend? What, precisely, have we been set free from? We cannot protect our liberty unless we understand exactly what it involves.

There are two great threats to Christian liberty: *legalism* on one side, and *licentiousness* on the other. All three of these crucial ideas (liberty, legalism, and licentiousness) are dealt with in Galatians 5, and each one helps explain the others.

Liberty

The average worldling thinks of religion as a confining, restrictive regimen of meritorious duties. Scripture portrays Christianity as just the opposite: a liberating, emancipating, bondage–breaking release from sin's bondage; acquittal from divine condemnation; and freedom from the necessity of earning God's favor.

Understanding Christian liberty as Scripture defines it is crucial. When Jesus spoke of freedom for captives and liberty to the oppressed, He was not describing something as mundane as political liberty for people under earthly tyranny. He was not planning the overthrow of the Roman government. As despotic and morally unrighteous as that system was, Christ never tried to foment a political revolution. He was not employing emancipation language the way today's radicals and purveyors of "liberation theology" typically do.

Instead, Jesus was speaking of *spiritual* liberty. This liberty is the birthright of every believer. It is a vast freedom from the yoke of any earthly, sinful, or Satanic bondage. It is the greatest, truest liberty imaginable. Two important aspects of Christian liberty must be kept in constant focus and in careful balance.

Freedom from the bondage of sin. Liberty in Christ is *not* freedom from spiritual responsibility. It is certainly not any kind of moral autonomy. It is not a release from the divine standard of righteousness. It does not mean we are discharged from our duty to obey the moral law. Those who think of Christian liberty in such terms are expressly condemned in Scripture. They use their freedom as a coverup for evil (1 Peter 2:16). They talk about freedom, "but they themselves are slaves of corruption" (2 Peter 2:19).

There's a name for that kind of thinking. The theological term for it is *antinomianism.* Antinomians believe our liberty in Christ releases us from any obligation to God's law, period. They typically cite Romans 6:14 ("You are not under law but under grace"), as if that verse meant no law or commandment has any binding authority whatsoever for the Christian—as if the principle of grace completely abrogated every standard ever set by the law. But Scripture specifically says grace teaches otherwise, "training us to renounce ungodliness and worldly passions, and to live self–controlled, upright, and godly lives in the present age" (Titus 2:12).

Don't ever think that the standard of righteousness revealed in God's law has been annulled or truncated. The moral content of the law will *never* be repealed because it is grounded in the very character of God. It is as eternal and immutable as He is.

For example, because God is truth, it is wrong to lie. Because God is just, it is sinful to murder or steal. Because God is love, it is unrighteous to covet or bear false witness. And because God is holy and all-powerful, it is blasphemy to have any other gods before him, to take His name in vain, or to worship a graven image—as if a piece of stone or wood could stand in His place. The laws prohibiting such evils reflect the holy, immutable character of God, and therefore the rules those commandments articulate are eternally binding. Theologians historically have referred to this as *the moral law—*

a standard of perfect righteousness that can never be repealed or nullified. It was surely not without significance that when God gave the law to Moses at Sinai, the first precepts handed down were the Ten Commandments, and they were inscribed on tablets of stone.

But there was never a time when the moral law was not in effect; it was binding on people long before God wrote the Decalogue at Sinai. That's why it was a sin for Cain to kill Abel. It was a sin for Pharaoh to covet Abraham's wife. It was a sin for Joseph's brothers to resent what he had, and to bear false witness against him. It was a sin for Nimrod and the Babylonians, Pharaoh and the Egyptians, to worship other gods. The moral principles delineated in the Ten Commandments were binding long before God wrote them on stone tablets.

In fact, God Himself made that very point when He gave the law to Israel. He told Moses, "Whoever does these things [the sins delineated there] is an abomination to the LORD. And because of these abominations the LORD your God is driving [the Canaanites] out before you" (Deuteronomy 18:12). In other words, God punished the pagan inhabitants of the land for violating His moral law even though, as far as we know from Scripture, no one had ever received any written commandments from God. But the moral precepts given in the law were clearly binding anyway, and God's punishment was severe.

Was that punishment just? Absolutely. Those people knew that what they did was wrong. A sense of right and wrong is an innate aspect of our humanity. Indeed, key elements of God's moral law are inscribed on every human heart by the Creator Himself, and every unseared human conscience testifies to that fact. That's why Cain was afraid to face God, and Joseph's brothers were afraid to face him. In Paul's words "when

Gentiles, who do not have the law, by nature do what the law requires, they are a law to themselves, even though they do not have the law. They show that the work of the law is written on their hearts, while their conscience also bears witness" (Romans 2:14–15).

That is why people who have never heard the gospel are nevertheless guilty. They have an innate understanding of enough moral law to condemn them, an inborn awareness of God, evidence of His attributes, which can be seen in nature, and enough spiritual sense to know that their Creator is a righteous Judge to whom they are accountable (Romans 1:18–20), but they sin anyway and deliberately suppress what they do know of God. "So they are without excuse" (v. 20).

How unchanging is the moral aspect of God's law? Consider this: God's perfect standard of righteousness will still govern our conduct and thinking even in heaven, where we will finally be able to obey God's righteous standard perfectly, with no inclination or desire to do otherwise. That, by the way, will be *the truest liberty of all,* when "the creation itself will be set free from its bondage to corruption and obtain the freedom of the glory of the children of God" (Romans 8:21).

Conversely, Scripture consistently teaches that freedom from righteousness is no freedom at all. The Apostle Paul says in Romans 6:20 that to be free from righteousness is to be enslaved to sin. Jesus said in John 8:34, "Everyone who commits sin is a slave to sin."

So this is the essential starting point for understanding what Christian liberty is all about: it is first of all freedom from the bondage of sin, and therefore it *cannot* be the kind of freedom that nullifies our obligation to the eternal principles of God's moral law.

When Paul writes, "You are not under law but under grace" in Romans 6:14, that is the culminating point in a long argument he has made *against* antinomianism. That chapter starts with Paul anticipating the antinomian argument: "What shall we say then? Are we to continue in sin that grace may abound? By no means! How can we who died to sin still live in it?" (vv. 1–2). He goes on to say that our union with Christ makes us participants in His death, "so that we would no longer be enslaved to sin. For one who has died has been set free from sin" (vv. 6–7). We're also participants in His resurrection (vv. 5, 8), raised to "walk in newness of life" (v. 4). Finally, the whole argument in Romans 6 is summarized with these words in Romans 6:17–18: "You who were once slaves of sin have become obedient from the heart to the standard of teaching to which you were committed, and, having been set free from sin, have become slaves of righteousness."

The true sense of Romans 6:14 cannot be correctly understood apart from that context. In fact, when set in its proper context it powerfully refutes antinomianism: *"Sin will have no dominion over you,* since you are not under law but under grace."

That verse is a perfect statement of the two aspects of Christian liberty. The first phrase declares that believers are free from the bondage of sin. Far from declaring the law's moral principles null and void, it is a triumphant celebration of victory over sin because "the righteous requirement of the law [is] fulfilled in us, who walk not according to the flesh but according to the Spirit" (Romans 8:1).

The second half of Romans 6:14 is talking about our deliverance from the *curse* and the *condemnation* of the law. Here is the second vital feature of our liberty in Christ.

Freedom from the yoke of the law. Paul's focus in Galatians 5 hones in mainly on this second aspect of Christian liberty. The point, again, is not that the law's moral demands have been eliminated, but that the curse and condemnation of the law have been lifted. The law is not a burden to believers the way it is to unbelievers—because Christ has born the law's condemnation on behalf of His people. All the onerous aspects of the law have thus been removed.

Paul therefore reminds the Galatians that they are no longer under the law's yoke. Verse 18 echoes the point he made in Romans 6: "If you are led by the Spirit, you are not under the law." Here we see yet again, that the phrase *"not under the law"* cannot mean that the moral principles of the law have been overturned or nullified, because Paul goes on (starting in the very next verse) to compare the works of the flesh with the fruit of the Spirit, making it clear that those who "walk by the Spirit . . . will not gratify the desires of the flesh" (v. 16).

The phrase *"not under the law"* is best explained by how Paul uses it elsewhere in this epistle. Just one chapter earlier, in Galatians 4:4–5, Paul wrote, "God sent forth his Son, born of woman, born *under the law,* to redeem those who were *under the law."* In that context, Paul is comparing the law to a tutor (v. 2). He goes on to say that because Christ has redeemed us, we have been adopted as God's sons, given the full privileges of adult sons, and released from the tutor's reproaches and severity.

That is a fitting picture of the kind of liberty Paul is describing. It is like the freedom of a son who comes of age. The law's threats, its harsh discipline, and some of its rigid measures (in particular, the dietary laws and ceremonial features) were temporary training measures—designed to point Israel toward Christ. But now that Christ has come, He has redeemed us from the tutelage of the law and given us the status of full-grown sons. We enjoy a freedom no one who lived under yoke of the law ever had.

What kind of freedom does this give us? Chiefly two benefits, one whose advantages are mainly temporal, the other whose value is vast and eternal.

First, *we're free from the law's complex ceremonies.* (This is the temporal benefit.) All the ceremonial aspects of the Old Testament law were prophetic types and pictures that pointed to Christ. In Colossians 2:16–17 Paul writes: "let no one pass judgment on you in questions of food and drink, or with regard to a festival or a new moon or a Sabbath. These are a shadow of the things to come, but the substance belongs to Christ." He identifies all the dietary laws, as well as the Sabbaths and feast days, as mere shadows of Christ—wispy, temporary features of the law that have been superseded by the reality they pointed to.

That includes all the *rituals* of Old Testament worship. They were illustrations that pointed to Christ; they foreshadowed Him. They all symbolized aspects of His person and work. The whole sacrificial system, for example, was an elaborate picture that foretold the atoning work of Christ in the most graphic, bloody imagery. But it was *just* imagery. Hebrews 10:4 says: "It is impossible for the blood of bulls and goats to take away sins." Constant, daily, ritual sacrifices were the main substance Old Testament liturgy and the primary activity of the priesthood. It was grueling, never-ending work, yet such things "can never take away sins" (Hebrews 10:11).

Those sacrifices vividly *pictured* the cost of redemption, but at the end of the day they were only shadows—utterly ineffectual in and of themselves to accomplish the work they pictured. Scripture is emphatic about this: "Since the law has but a shadow of the good things to come instead of the true form of these realities, it can never, by the same sacrifices that are continually offered every year, make perfect those who draw near" (Hebrews 10:1).

But Christ completely fulfilled the promise represented by the Temple sacrifices when He offered Himself once for all and shed His own blood on the cross. To retreat to those shadows and put oneself under obligation to the ceremonies of Old Testament religion would be like turning one's back on the living person of Christ and worshiping His shadow instead.

That's exactly the kind of threat those false teachers in Galatia represented. They wanted to preserve the ceremonial elements of Old Covenant, starting with circumcision. (In effect they were teaching that it is impossible to be justified through faith in Christ without first being circumcised.) Their doctrine was a *de facto* denial of the efficacy of Christ's sacrifice.

Paul has them in mind in Galatians 5:2–3 when he says: "Look: I, Paul, say to you that if you accept circumcision, Christ will be of no advantage to you. I testify again to every man who accepts circumcision that he is obligated to keep the whole law." In other words, if you want to ignore Christ and retreat to the shadows of Old Covenant ceremony, then you have made yourself a slave to the whole law.

Incidentally, Paul wasn't ruling out the salvation of already-circumcised Jews in verse 2. He was writing to *Gentiles* who were tempted to undergo circumcision as a prerequisite to justification. He was telling them that if any point of law is a prerequisite to justification, then the *whole* law is also binding.

See, if our justification hinges in any degree on a righteousness we gain from our own obedience, then that obedience must be perfect in every respect, because the law demands perfect obedience and pronounces a full and final condemnation on anyone who violates any point of it. "For whoever keeps the whole law but fails in one point has become accountable for all of it" (James 2:10). Partial obedience to the law does not result in a partial righteousness. Partial obedience is *dis*obedience, and that is *un*righteousness, so it is of no value for our justification.

Are Christians free to observe Old Testament ceremonies—say, the feast days and festivals—as long as we don't regard such things as necessary, meritorious, or instruments of justification? Certainly (Romans 14:5–6; Colossians 2:16–17). Timothy (whose father was Greek) was circumcised after becoming a Christian in order to avoid controversy when he ministered in a Jewish community. Paul himself took a Nazarite vow (Acts 18:18), and on another occasion participated in a purification ceremony (Acts 21:26). But when ministering among Gentiles he made no effort to keep kosher. Paul thus used his freedom to avoid unnecessary offense to either Jews or Gentiles. He expressly spelled out his philosophy in 1 Corinthians 9:19–22:

> For though I am free from all, I have made myself a servant to all, that I might win more of them. To the Jews I became as a Jew, in order to win Jews. To those under the law I became as one under the law (though not being myself under the law) that I might win those under the law. To those outside the law I became as one outside the law (not being outside the law of God but under the law of Christ) that I might win those outside the law. To the weak I became weak, that I might win the weak. I have become all things to all people, that by all means I might save some.

But note that Paul is talking about something that is optional and totally voluntary. The rigid, obligatory observance of the law's dietary laws, feast days, and cleansing ceremonies has been done away with the institution of a new and better covenant. Furthermore, the sacrificial system has been completely eliminated—or rather perfectly fulfilled. We are no longer under the yoke of Old Covenant ceremonies.

The second benefit of being "not under law" is even more important: *We are free from the Law's fatal curse.* This is the vast, eternal benefit of Christian liberty.

The law is a killer. It could never justify sinners. It can only condemn; it cannot save. It is full of threats and judgments for those who fail to keep it perfectly. That is the curse of the law. There is not a single word of encouragement anywhere in the entire law for sinners who hope to earn enough merit through their own legal obedience to eliminate their guilt and gain the righteousness they need for a right standing with God. As we have seen, the law demands perfect obedience. Even the sacrifices prescribed in the law were symbolic only, offering no real atonement. Everyone under the law who sins is condemned, full stop.

Even in the Old Testament the only hope sinners had for being justified was by the imputation of a righteousness that was not their own. Abraham "believed the LORD, and He counted it to him as righteousness" (Genesis 15:6). "David also speaks of the blessing of the one to whom God counts righteousness apart from works" (Romans 4:6). Even in the Old Covenant era, people were not saved by their legal obedience. The only way any sinner has ever been redeemed is by grace through faith. "For all who rely on works of the law are under a curse; for it is written, 'Cursed be everyone who does not abide by all things written in the Book of the Law, and do them.' Now it is evident that no one is justified before God by the law, for 'The righteous shall live by faith' " (Galatians 3:10–11).

The Jewish legalists who had sowed confusion among the Galatians didn't even understand their own Old Testament. They believed obedience to the law could gain them a righteousness that would become the ground of their justification before God. Paul says that is a damning lie. To those tempted to follow such an error the apostle writes, "You are severed from Christ, you who would be justified by the law; you have fallen away from grace" (5:4).

This was the gist of the Judaizers' error: They thought they could be justified by law. They had missed the whole point of the law, which is to condemn sinners and leave them with no hope but the grace of God.

But "Christ redeemed us from the curse of the law by becoming a curse for us." (Galatians 3:13). He took the guilt of our sin and was punished in our place. Best of all, His perfect righteousness—exactly what the law demands—is imputed to us. We are credited with His flawless obedience. So the curse of the law is totally and eternally eliminated for all who believe.

It should be clear by now that Christian liberty is not a one dimensional concept. It is a glorious liberty from the bondage of sin, and it's also a welcome deliverance from the yoke of the law. The Apostle Paul has both aspects of liberty in view when he says (v. 1): "be not entangled again with the yoke of bondage"—neither bondage to sin nor bondage to the law. To go back under the yoke of the law again is the error of *legalism,* and to go back under the yoke of sin is the error of *licentiousness.* Before we close this chapter, we need to take note of what Galatians 5 says about those two kinds of bondage.

Legalism

Legalism, of course, was the central error of the Galatian Judaizers. Theirs was a deadly brand of legalism, because it destroyed the doctrine of justification by faith. They made circumcision an essential instrument of justification rather than faith alone.

Roman Catholicism makes a very similar error. According to Rome, the imputed righteousness of Christ is not a sufficient ground for justification. Catholic Popes and councils have devised a multitude of rituals, sacraments, and superstitions through which they claim people can earn merit for themselves and thereby supplement the atoning work of Christ—as if Christ's work were deficient. In the Roman system, therefore, the believer's own works, starting with baptism, are necessary instruments of justification. That is exactly the same kind of legalism Paul condemned in his epistle to the Galatians.

In Galatians 5:6, the apostle expressly points to faith as the sole instrument of justification: "In Christ Jesus neither circumcision nor uncircumcision counts for anything, but *only faith [sola fide]* working through love." Whether someone is circumcised or not is immaterial to the question of whether he is justified. We lay hold of justification by faith alone—specifically, *faith that works by love.* In other words, the true faith through which God justifies is not a notional faith that obeys mechanically because of laws and rituals and external motives. It is a hearty faith that inevitably expresses itself in genuine love—earnest love for God first of all, and active love for others as well (*cf.* 1 John 4:7–8).

Works—even works that are the fruit of genuine love—can never be the ground of our justification. Our very best works are still imperfect and impure and tinged with mixed motives. The only righteousness that God receives is a perfect righteousness, and the only way to be credited with a perfect righteousness is to have Christ's righteousness imputed to us by faith.

Paul had high hopes that the Galatians had truly received the gospel by faith, despite their confusion on this issue. He writes in verses 7–10: "You were running well. Who hindered you from obeying the truth? This persuasion is not from Him who calls you. A little leaven leavens the whole lump. I have confidence in the Lord that you will take no other view than mine, and the one who is troubling you will bear the penalty, whoever he is." In other words, while Paul was optimistic about the faith of the Galatian believers, he believed that those who were teaching this legalistic gospel would be judged by God—which is to say that he did not even regard the Judaizers as authentic Christians. That's why he pronounced such a harsh anathema on them in Galatians 1:8–9. Clearly, the Apostle Paul regarded legalism as the very worst kind of apostasy.

Even harsher words for the heretics were yet to come. Verse 11 implies that the Judaizers had falsely assured the Galatians that Paul agreed with their teaching. He is emphatic in his denial: "If I, brothers, still preach circumcision, why am I still being persecuted? In that case the offense of the cross has been removed" (v. 11). Not only did he not agree with their teaching, he regarded it as a fatal compromise and a denial of the gospel's core truth.

Then he adds this: "I wish those who unsettle you would emasculate themselves!" (v. 12). If the legalists thought circumcision was something meritorious, why not go even further, like some of the pagan cults did, and turn themselves into eunuchs? There's no delicate way of paraphrasing Paul's point, because he was not trying to be delicate. If the Judaizers believed removal of a Gentile's foreskin earned favor with God, then they ought to take their doctrine to its logical end and castrate themselves!

That is some of the harshest language Paul uses anywhere in the New Testament. It shows what a serious error legalism is.

Licentiousness

Still, legalism is by no means the only danger to Christian liberty. There's another kind of bondage that destroys true liberty in Christ: bondage to sin. If legalism is the error of abandoning our liberty in Christ in order to return to the yoke of the law, licentiousness is the error of abandoning our liberty in Christ in order to return to the bondage of sin.

Both errors are equally grave. Both are utterly destructive to authentic Christian liberty. And yet it is quite common to hear professing Christians justify the practice of some favorite sin by an appeal to the principle of Christian liberty. "I'm free in Christ," they say, as if Christ bought us freedom to indulge in fleshly activities rather than deliverance from such things.

Paul condemns that very error in the very same context where he is arguing against legalism: "For you were called to freedom, brothers. Only do not use your freedom as an opportunity for the flesh" (Galatians 5:13). Three verses later he adds, "But I say, walk by the Spirit, and you will not gratify the desires of the flesh."

In between those two statements, Paul highlights a simple principle that is the key to understanding this whole issue. Here's what Paul says is the antidote to licentiousness: "Through love serve one another. For the whole law is fulfilled in one word: 'You shall love your neighbor as yourself' " (vv. 13–14). He says virtually the same thing in Romans 13:8: "The one who loves another has fulfilled the law"; and again in Romans 13:10: "Love is the fulfilling of the law."

Notice that love *fulfills* the law; it does not nullify it. We've already stressed the truth that the moral demands of the law are eternal and can never be nullified. But let's revisit that point one more time, because a lot of people seem to have the mistaken impression that the teaching of Christ and the apostles *nullified* the moral precepts of Old Testament law and replaced them with the principle of love. I frequently encounter people who want to justify a casual attitude toward God's moral law by claiming that all the moral precepts of the Old Testament have all been eliminated and replaced with a single, much simpler, New Commandment: love.

After all, Jesus *did* say, "A new commandment I give to you, that you love one another" (John 13:34).

But that does not *nullify* the righteous standard of the law. It simply comprehends and encompasses the whole moral content of the law in a single commandment. That's why in 1 John 2:7–8 the Apostle John says: "Beloved, I am writing you no new commandment, but an old commandment that you had from the beginning. The old commandment is the word that you have heard. At the same time, it is a new commandment." It is a *New* Commandment only in the sense that it was renewed and magnified and given its proper place of prominence by Christ. It is certainly not new with respect to the duties it commits us to. It is actually an old commandment and was included in Moses' law all along: "You shall love the LORD your God with all your heart and with all your soul and with all your might" (Deuteronomy 6:5) and, "You shall love your neighbor as yourself" (Leviticus 19:18). But love is a perfect summary statement of the whole moral law.

Moreover, the principle of love gets to the heart of our motivation for obeying the law. If we isolate the specific statements of the moral law and take the surface meaning of the commandments only (don't steal, don't kill, don't commit adultery), it's relatively easy to obey the law in its external, superficial mandate. The Pharisees were highly skilled at doing that while indulging in all kinds of evil imaginations in their hearts. What *really* fulfills the moral law is not a mere wooden adherence to the external commandments, but sincere love for God and for one another. When we get to the heart of the moral law, that is precisely what every commandment demands of us: love. The specific moral precepts simply define in detail what true love will do.

So the core and the anchor of all the moral precepts of God's law boil down to one simple commandment: love. That's not something that can ever be turned into an empty ritual or a mere external show. That one commandment goes straight to the heart.

And here's the key: The Holy Spirit is the only source of the love that fulfills the law. "Walk by the Spirit, and you will not gratify the desires of the flesh" (v. 16).

That truth is the very foundation of our liberty in Christ. The Holy Spirit enables us to love, and that liberates us to fulfill the righteousness of God's moral law.

That is the purest kind of liberty. It is a freedom to love God, to please Him, and to obey Him from a pure heart.

Real Love and Real Liberty

Phil Johnson

Do not use your freedom as an opportunity for the flesh, but through love serve one another. For the whole law is fulfilled in one word: "You shall love your neighbor as yourself." Galatians 5:13–14

The legalist masquerades as a lover of the law, but in reality he turns the law on its head. "For the commandments, 'You shall not commit adultery, You shall not murder, You shall not steal, You shall not covet,' and any other commandment, are summed up in this word: 'You shall love your neighbor as yourself' " (Romans 13:9). Scripture furthermore says the law of Christ is best fulfilled when we "bear one another's burdens" (Galatians 6:2).

By contrast, legalism weighs people down with burdens too heavy to be borne. It adds man-made rules to the precepts of Scripture. It saddles God's people with duties He never commanded. It tries to make self look better by magnifying others' shame. That is the exact antithesis of love. There is no more egregious way of twisting and corrupting the true intent of God's law.

Two Kinds of Legalism

People who like to bind others' consciences with their own rules and restrictions sometimes defend themselves against charges of legalism with a clever diversionary tactic. True *legalism*, they say, is the brand of false teaching Paul condemned in Galatians 1—the error of making some prerequisite work or religious ceremony a condition of justification. By that narrow definition, a *legalist* is someone who believes in salvation by works. Therefore, they say, as long as you formally affirm the principle of *sola fide* (faith as the sole instrument of justification), you can't legitimately be labeled a legalist, no matter how many rules you make and impose on people who are already converted.

A better definition of legalism would be one that echoes Galatians 5:1. *Legalism* is the error of abandoning our liberty in Christ in order to take on a yoke of legal bondage in the hope that this will earn merit or gain favor with God. There are actually *two* flavors of legalism expressly condemned in Scripture.

First is the one recognized and despised even by the strict fundamentalist with his thick rule-book. It's *the legalism of the Judaizers*. The Judaizers wanted to make circumcision a requirement for salvation. They had fatally corrupted the gospel by adding a human work as a requirement for salvation. That is certainly the *worst* variety of legalism, because it destroys the doctrine of justification by faith and thereby sets up "a gospel contrary to the one you received" (Galatians 1:8–9). According to the Apostle Paul, that kind of legalist is not an authentic Christian.

But another kind of legalism is *the legalism of the Pharisees*. It's the tendency to measure spirituality by a list of manmade rules. This kind of legalism is a common pitfall even within the household of faith. At the root of Pharisaical legalism is a belief that holiness is achieved by legal means—living one's life by rigorous rules and restrictions: "Do not handle, Do not taste, Do not touch" (Colossians 2:20–22). This type of legalism doesn't necessarily destroy the doctrine of justification like the legalism of the Judaizers. But it does significant damage to the doctrine of sanctification, and it is certainly appropriate to call it what it is: *legalism*. It is a sinful misapplication of law, an attempt to make law do work that only grace can do. Like the

Judaizers' brand of legalism, it brings people under a yoke of bondage Scripture has not placed on them.

As a matter of fact, that is exactly what Jesus said about the legalism of the Pharisees: "They tie up heavy burdens, hard to bear, and lay them on people's shoulders" (Matthew 23:4).

The Folly of Going Beyond What Is Written

Pharisaical legalists are not content to live life in the power of the Spirit, cultivate discernment, and avoid activities that are clearly profane or immoral; they make lists of rules that prohibit Christians from practically everything but church activities. They think it's not sufficient to do things in moderation and exercise self-control; they make rules that call for strict abstinence from everything doubtful. And they try to impose their rules on other Christians—saddling people with a yoke that they have dreamed up out of somewhere in the white spaces of Scripture.

Want rules? Here's a good one to start with: *On the subject of spiritual duties, where Scripture stops speaking, we should, too.*

The Pharisees' sin was making rules that went beyond Scripture. For example, they read in the law that it is a sin to take God's name in vain (Exodus 20:7), so they expanded the rule to forbid the use of God's name at all. They invented euphemisms to be used in place of God's name (Matthew 23:22).

They saw the stress that was laid on ceremonial cleanness in the Old Testament, so they invented all kinds of extra washings and required people to perform them—as if these were divinely-ordained sacraments. In fact, Matthew 15 tells how they tried to condemn even Jesus for not making his disciples observe their extrabiblical traditions: "Pharisees and scribes came to Jesus from Jerusalem and said, 'Why do your disciples break the tradition of the elders? For they do not wash their hands when they eat' " (Matthew 15:1–2).

There was no biblical commandment requiring a ceremonial washing before someone ate. The priests were supposed to wash their hands before offering sacrifices to God, but no law required everyone to wash up before every meal. The institution of such an ordinance as if it were a sacred duty was a classic case of Pharisaical legalism, and Jesus abominated the practice.

In fact, Jesus' response to the Pharisees was a stern rebuke: "He answered them, 'And why do you break the commandment of God for the sake of your tradition?' " (Matthew 15:3). In other words, He rejected their tradition *because it was not what the Word of God taught.* Even though it may be quite true that washing before meals is good hygiene and therefore generally a good idea—and Jesus certainly knew that—He flatly rejected the Pharisees' insistence that it is "sinful" *not* to do it.

Notice, He said their legalism transgressed the Scriptures. Legalism always has an anti-biblical tendency. You cannot go *beyond* Scripture without ultimately setting yourself *at odds with* Scripture.

That is precisely what happened in the fundamentalist movement of the twentieth century, and it is one of the major reasons that movement failed so notoriously. Legalism diverts people's attention from sound doctrine. So the fundamentalist movement was soon plagued with appalling doctrinal ignorance. The typical fundamentalist reserved his or her strongest convictions for a culture-bound system of manmade rules, which in effect took the place of fundamental doctrines in their thinking.

Ask the typical self-proclaimed fundamentalist to define the difference between imputed and imparted righteousness, and he will not be able to do so. Suggest that it's okay to use a Bible translation other than the King James Version, or accidentally violate some other manmade fundamentalist taboo, and you will find he is already locked and loaded with angry dogmatism, ready to do battle for his tradition. As Jesus said of the Pharisees, they have nullified the Word of God for the sake of their man-made system. They neglect the truly fundamental doctrines of Christianity in favor of their own contrived standards and specious dress codes.

I once had a protracted discussion with a fundamentalist pastor who insisted that it is a sin to listen to contemporary music because so much of it is loud and rhythmic. Loud volume and a strong beat are the two elements of today's music that appeal most to the flesh, he said. He insisted it is perfectly evident to any truly spiritual person that noisy music and syncopated rhythms are inherently sinful. He dismissed the percussion instruments named in Psalm 150 (especially the "loud clashing cymbals") as relics of Old Covenant worship. When I suggested that the psalm nevertheless challenges his axiom that rhythm *per se* is self-evidently sinful, he angrily ended the conversation.

Whatever one's tastes in music styles, Scripture clearly teaches that it is a very serious sin to impose on others any "spiritual" standard that has no biblical basis. When God gave the law to Israel, He told them, "You shall not add to the word that I command you, nor take from it, that you may keep the commandments of the LORD your God that I command you" (Deuteronomy 4:2). "Everything that I command you, you shall be careful to do. You shall not add to it or take from it" (Deuteronomy 12:32).

The same principle is repeated in the New Testament. We find in 1 Corinthians 4 Paul rebuking the Corinthians for their sectarianism, saying "I am of Paul"; "I am of Apollos," and so on. His rebuke to them includes these words in 1 Corinthians 4:6: "I have applied all these things to myself and Apollos for your benefit, brothers, *that you may learn by us not to go beyond what is written.*"

That is a good guideline for how we should exercise our Christian liberty: Don't go beyond what is written in Scripture. Don't make rules to impose on others; don't devise rituals and forms of worship that are not authorized; and don't speak on such matters where God has been silent. That's how the principle of *Sola Scriptura* applies to Christian living. If we really believe Scripture is a sufficient rule for sanctification, then we don't have to add anything to it.

Nor is there virtue in applying every principle of Scripture in the strictest possible way. "Keep[ing] oneself unstained from the world" (James 1:27) doesn't mean you have to avoid contact with the world or retreat to a nunnery (1 Corinthians 5:9–12). If we add rules that Scripture doesn't make—especially if we try to impose our man-made rules on other people's consciences as a standard of spirituality—we are guilty of the same sin as the Pharisees and worthy of the same harsh rebukes Christ leveled at them.

A Test Case: Food Offered to Idols

Love is not only the fulfillment of the law; it is also the only context in which Christian liberty can function properly. The Apostle Paul actually had quite a lot to say about how to exercise Christian liberty in love.

There was a debate in the Corinthian church about whether Christian liberty extended to an issue like eating food that had been offered on pagan altars. Corinth was full of temples where food was placed in honor of various Roman gods. Pagan priests would then sell that food in local markets, and that is how they made a living. Many of the Corinthians were converts from that kind of paganism and had scruples about eating food that had been ceremoniously dedicated to pagan idols. Evidently, there were others in the church who did not agree with the concern. (Perhaps this difference grew out of economic necessity; food from the temples was sold at a discount.) So the church had written to ask Paul for an apostolic ruling on the question.

He responded with an answer that must have surprised those repelled by pagan worship: He told them an idol is nothing (1 Corinthians 8:4), and Christians are free to eat food offered to idols; it is an utterly indifferent matter. "We are no worse off if we do not eat, and no better off if we do" (v. 8).

But that was not the end of Paul's answer. He went on to warn at length against the danger of using our liberty in a way that hurts others. "Take care that this right of yours does not somehow become a stumbling block to the weak" (v. 9). Christian liberty is not to be used in a selfish way, but always in consideration of others. Paul said, "If food makes my brother stumble, I will never eat meat, lest I make my brother stumble" (v. 13). That verse marks the end of chapter 8, and all of chapter 9 is Paul's testimony of how he gave up various aspects of His own personal liberty for the sake of the gospel. "Though I am free from all, I have made myself a servant to all, that I might win more of them" (9:19). "I have become all things to all people, that by all means I might save some" (v. 22).

The theme of chapter 10 is still Christian liberty and how to use it responsibly. Paul reminds the Corinthians of Old Testament Israel, and how they fell into idolatry through a combination of overconfident carelessness and carnal worldliness. He makes it plain that his approval of eating food offered to idols does not constitute approval of idolatry itself. In fact, he says, "Flee from idolatry" (10:14). He reminds the

Corinthians that evils such as false worship, immorality, and complaining against God are not matters of Christian liberty; they are outright sins.

That context is crucial. When Paul says "all things are lawful" in verse 23, we can be certain he is not teaching that Christians have liberty to do the things he had just condemned as sinful. On the contrary, he seems to be quoting a phrase that some of the Corinthians were using to justify selfish abuses of their Christian liberty—and he emphatically disagrees with their abuse of that principle.

Remember, the question that launched this section of 1 Corinthians was about food. As far as food is concerned, it is quite true that "all things are lawful" (*cf.* 1 Corinthians 6:12–13; Mark 7:19; Romans 14: 14–15). At times, however, love demands that we abstain from eating certain things for the sake of others.

Paul was writing to people who were prone to use their liberty for self-serving ends. So near the end of 1 Corinthians 10, as he wraps up that lengthy answer to their question about food offered to idols, he gives three principles that will correct that selfish tendency. Each one is a reminder of how liberty is to be exercised in love.

Our Liberty Is for the Good of Others

First, he urges the Corinthians to use their liberty in an unselfish manner.

When the gospel was under attack at the hands of Judaizing legalists in Galatia, Paul urged believers to stand fast in defense of their liberty (Galatians 5:1). When false teachers are undermining fundamental truths of the gospel, no concessions are to be made.

When he writes to the Corinthians, however, Paul says there is a time when the right thing to do is to forgo the exercise of one's personal liberties for the good of our own brothers and sisters.

Paul was concerned with those who had weak consciences, people recently saved out of paganism who were fearful of eating foods that had been offered to the very idols they formerly worshiped. Even though it was *lawful* for them to eat any food that could be purchased in Corinth, they did not fully understand their liberty. Their consciences were uneasy. They feared potential defilement if they ate anything that had been used in idol worship. Therefore, since they could not eat with a pure conscience, it would indeed be a sin *for them* to eat such food. As Paul wrote in Romans 14:23: "Whoever has doubts is condemned if he eats, because the eating is not from faith. For whatever does not proceed from faith is sin." It's a sin to go against one's own conscience, even when the conscience is misinformed.

It is likewise a sin, and a gross breach of Christian charity, to influence someone with a weak conscience to go against his conscience. Christian liberty is never to be flaunted in a way that injures the weaker brother. The Apostle Paul was keenly aware of that danger, and he strongly cautioned the Corinthians about it:

"If anyone sees you who have knowledge eating in an idol's temple, will he not be encouraged, if his conscience is weak, to eat food offered to idols? And so by your knowledge this weak person is destroyed, the brother for whom Christ died. Thus, sinning against your brothers and wounding their conscience when it is weak, you sin against Christ. Therefore, if food makes my brother stumble, I will never eat meat, lest I make my brother stumble" (1 Corinthians 8:10–13).

As believers we have absolute liberty to do anything we like, as long as it does not conflict with the eternal moral principles of God. If a thing is not either explicitly or implicitly condemned in Scripture, we are free to do it.

But we are not supposed to use our freedom in a way that harms others. Lots of things that are legal are nonetheless not edifying. When Paul makes that statement in 1 Corinthians 10:23, he has in mind primarily what edifies *others*. If a thing hurts my brother rather than building him up, I must forgo my freedom. "Let no one seek his own good, but the good of his neighbor" (1 Corinthians 10:24).

Paul is not suggesting it's okay to nurture a weak conscience. He's not forbidding mature Christians to instruct those with weak consciences about what is lawful and what is not. In fact, the goal of the exercise is to "build up" the weaker brother (v. 23). But Paul is saying in that fleeting moment when you are confronted with a choice, it is right to defer to the weaker brother's scruples. In the course of your subsequent ministry to that brother, it may be helpful to instruct him in the truth of Scripture so that the Word of God can strengthen his conscience. But when he is struggling with the choice, your duty is to help guard his tender conscience, even if that means you must temporarily relinquish your personal liberty.

If his conscience is emboldened by seeing you eat the food he thinks is sinful to eat, so that he eats without understanding the biblical reasons why what he thought was sinful is not, then you have hurt him. You have caused him to defile his own conscience. You have wounded your brother for the sake of your own liberty. That is an abuse, not a legitimate expression, of Christian liberty.

Later, however, after he is instructed from Scripture, and he sees from the Word of God why eating that food is no sin at all—once his conscience is thus strengthened and enlightened by the truth of God's Word and he is fully persuaded in his own mind—*then* if he eats the food, you have not caused him to sin in doing so.

The point is to do what edifies. In the moment of making a choice, that often means surrendering your own freedom. Over the long haul, that means instructing the weaker brother about the truth of Christian liberty.

In fact, Paul himself underscores once more his original answer to the Corinthians' question: *there is no sin in eating food offered to idols.* He writes: "Eat whatever is sold in the meat market without raising any question on the ground of conscience. For 'the earth is the Lord's, and the fullness thereof' " (vv. 25–26). A believer should not have a troubled conscience about such things. It is no mark of piety to abstain unnecessarily or to question every tiny thing for conscience' sake. "Everything created by God is good, and nothing is to be rejected if it is received with thanksgiving, for it is made holy by the word of God and prayer" (1 Timothy 4:4–5). "To the pure, all things are pure, but to the defiled and unbelieving, nothing is pure; but both their minds and their consciences are defiled" (Titus 1:15). "God . . . richly provides us with everything to enjoy" (1 Timothy 6:17).

Nevertheless, Paul says, a mature Christian should defer to the weakness of a young believer's conscience, because one primary way for us to make the most of our liberty is by seeking the good of others.

Our Liberty Is for the Growth of the Gospel

A second way to get the maximum spiritual benefit from our liberty in Christ is to use it for the advancement of the gospel. Paul stressed the evangelistic benefits of Christian liberty. For him, freedom in Christ was an important tool that needed to be employed for the growth and furtherance of the gospel, and he did this conscientiously: "I try to please everyone in everything I do, not seeking my own advantage, but that of many, that they may be saved" (v. 33).

This is actually an extension of the first principle. We should use our liberty for the good of others. And one of the greatest ways we can seek others' welfare is to govern our behavior in a way that will make the gospel as clear and as attractive as possible.

Paul elaborated on this same principle a chapter earlier:

> Though I am free from all, I have made myself a servant to all, that I might win more of them. To the Jews I became as a Jew, in order to win Jews. To those under the law I became as one under the law (though not being myself under the law) that I might win those under the law. To those outside the law I became as one outside the law (not being outside the law of God but under the law of Christ) that I might win those outside the law. To the weak I became weak, that I might win the weak. I have become all things to all people, that by all means I might save some. I do it all for the sake of the gospel, that I may share with them in its blessings (1 Corinthians 9:19-23).

Of course the Apostle Paul was not merely looking for the favor of men. In Galatians 1:10 he wrote: "Am I now seeking the approval of man, or of God? Or am I trying to please man? If I were still trying to please man, I would not be a servant of Christ." When he says in 1 Corinthians 10:33, "I try to please everyone in everything I do," he certainly isn't advocating any adjustment to the gospel to remove the offense of the cross. He wasn't condoning ear-tickling preaching.

Indeed, he says, "I do it all for the sake of the gospel" (1 Corinthians 9:23). His goal was to advance the gospel, not adapt it to the tastes of his audience. So this has nothing to do with the kind of compromise that is frequently labeled "contextualization" nowadays. Paul is talking about sacrificing his own liberty for the good of others and for the growth of the gospel. He would not sacrifice the message, but he *would* sacrifice himself to win people to Christ. He would give up his liberty completely—even become "a slave to all"—if that would promote the spread of the gospel.

Our Liberty Is for the Glory of God

Having said all that, Paul makes clear that the ultimate purpose for Christian liberty, and the highest end to which we can apply it, is for the glory of God. "Whether you eat or drink, or whatever you do, do all to the glory of God" (1 Corinthians 10:31).

Here's the most important of all lessons about Christian liberty: *Everything we can lawfully do may be done and should be done for the glory of God.* A parallel passage in Colossians 3:17 sheds even more light on the principle: "Whatever you do, in word or deed, do everything in the name of the Lord Jesus, giving thanks to God the Father through Him." In other words, every activity you can legitimately thank God for, you should do in the name of Christ and to the glory of God. That is the very pinnacle of Christian liberty.

Those words ("do all to the glory of God") are familiar. But have you ever thought about the sweeping extent of that commandment? It's saying that every non-sinful activity of our lives is an occasion to give God glory. Every breath we take, every task we perform—all of life is to be lived with God's glory in view.

Liberty to Be a Servant

There's an interesting paradox associated with true liberty in Christ, and Paul states it explicitly in 1 Corinthians 9:19: "Though I be free from all men, yet have I made myself servant unto all."

That's every Christian's responsibility as a free person. Christ has liberated from sin and redeemed us from the law's condemnation. Although free, we are now slaves of a different sort—captives under a new, joyful bondage. We are "servants [diakonos] of a new covenant, not of the letter, but of the Spirit" (2 Corinthians 3:6, NASB). "Having been freed from sin, [we] became slaves of righteousness" (Romans 6:18). We are now "slaves of Christ, doing the will of God from the heart" (Ephesians 6:6). We have given up the yoke of the law and the bondage of sin, but we are now slaves of Christ.

Even though His yoke is easy and the burden is light— even though God Himself supplies the strength by which we render our service—it is nonetheless portrayed in Scripture as slavery. As Christ's willing slaves, we voluntarily restrict our own liberty for others' sakes.

That is precisely what Jesus Himself modeled and encouraged. "If anyone would be first, he must be last of all and servant of all" (Mark 9:35).

No liberty is absolute. Everyone is enslaved to something and free from something. In the words of Romans 6:20–22: "When you were slaves of sin, you were free in regard to righteousness. But what fruit were you getting at that time from the things of which you are now ashamed? For the end of those things is death. But now that you have been set free from sin and have become slaves of God, the fruit you get leads to sanctification and its end, eternal life." Christian liberty is not anything like moral autonomy. Don't ever get the idea that you freedom in Christ means you are free from responsibility or out from under authority.

But real freedom from sin means enslavement to righteousness. That freedom will finally reach full fruition in heaven, when at last we will be able to obey the will of God without any inclination to do otherwise.

What Freedom From the Law Accomplishes For the Local Church

Jim Elliff

Without question, the blending of the Jewish and Greek cultures within the churches was the most urgent problem confronting Christ's apostles after Pentecost. Imagine what this was like for new believers in the first century. The Jew who had despised the unclean Gentile was now expected to sit at the table and to share the cup with him. Misunderstandings about the place of the Law and the customs surrounding it ignited relational problems between Jews and Gentiles who came to Christ. What should be the status of the Old Covenant Law in the life of the nascent churches, with all its purity commands, Sabbath days, and circumcision?

Consider how often Paul concerned himself with the problem of legalism, the use of the "works of the Law" for saving purposes, in his letters to the churches. When he wrote to Rome and Ephesus, the issue was thematic, as in other letters. One could easily express the burden of his Roman letter in these simple words: *the absolute impartiality of God.* Jews and Gentiles face the same wrath of God because they are all alike under sin, and they are also offered the same access to God because, in Christ, God is absolutely impartial toward ethnicity. The cross of Christ removed the barrier of the Law, bringing Jews and Gentiles together in Him. For Paul, the important historical figure is Abraham, not Moses. He was the "father of many nations" through Christ.

The Jewish man who had become a believer in Christ has

to look the Gentile in the face and say, "I love you," and vice versa, because God had now made them one. And the Jew-born Christian's insistence on Gentiles adopting their law-works and customs must end. Acceptance must reign. The old legalism no longer divided Jews from Gentiles. This is where the battle regarding legalism was principally fought, in my view. And the implications are enormous for us today.

Paul's Burden for Ephesus

In Ephesians, Paul states that through revelation he (along with Christ's apostles and prophets) had come to understand that the exclusive blessings thought to be the birthright of the ethnic Jews were not exclusively theirs, and that Gentiles were now "brought near" through the cross. Contemplate his words as he explains something of the "mystery" now revealed:

> By referring to this, when you read you can under-
> stand my insight into the mystery of Christ, which
> in other generations was not made known to the
> sons of men, as it has now been revealed to His holy
> apostles and prophets in the Spirit; to be specific,
> that the Gentiles are fellow heirs and fellow mem-
> bers of the body, and fellow partakers of the prom-
> ise in Christ Jesus through the gospel . . . (Ephesians
> 3:1–6 NASB)

This was no peripheral issue for Paul. It was his mission as the "apostle to the Gentiles," and it is the universal church's mission as well, to promote that harmony of cultures in Christ that the cross brings them (or, we might say, forces upon them for their good). The church must embrace diversity by becom-ing the one New Man through Christ and do everything possi-ble to live out that unity.

He was called to show the "administration of God" in the blessing to "all" who believe, Jew or Gentile, as seen in the promise to Abraham, "All the nations shall be blessed in you"

(Galatians 3:8). Imagine what it took for this former Jewish leader to accept that the Jews' lofty position as God's chosen people is not finally about ethnic Jews, but Jewish Christians sharing the position with "Gentile dogs" who have also become Christians. The promises made to the Jews are for all who are in Christ; the inheritance is both for Jews and Gentiles.

The immensity of this new knowledge is not only enough to cause every God-fearing Jew to scream curses at Paul, yet it is the very reason Gentiles have any hope whatsoever. Paul carried this message everywhere.

This homogeneity of Christian Jews and Gentiles was not a back-up plan but was fully intended by God from the beginning. Paul declares that all of this was "in accordance with the eternal purpose which He carried out in Christ Jesus our Lord" (Ephesians 3:11). The phrase "carried out" signifies completed action; it has to do with the finished work of the cross through which Christ destroyed the barrier between Gentiles and Jews who are in Christ. That barrier was the Law, as is seen below. Perhaps Paul was alluding to the Soreg, or wall of separation in the Temple courtyard, beyond which all Gentiles were denied access upon pain of death:

> But now in Christ Jesus you who formerly were far off have been brought near by the blood of Christ. For He Himself is our peace, who made both groups into one and broke down the barrier of the dividing wall, by abolishing in His flesh the enmity, which is the Law of commandments contained in ordinances, so that in Himself He might make the two [Christian Jew and Gentile] into one new man, thus establishing peace, and might reconcile them both in one body to God through the cross, by it having put to death the enmity (Ephesians 3:13–16 NASB).

There is so much talk of oneness in the New Testament that I can speak of it only in an introductory way. I am only calling attention to this idea by pointing to this massive stone that is laid in the bedrock of our Christianity. God took the most diverse cultures in existence and brought them together into an entirely new culture. From now on there is no "distinction between Greek and Jew, circumcised and uncircumcised, barbarian, Scythian, slave and freeman, but Christ is all, and in all" (Colossians 3:11). Jewish/Gentile oneness in Christ is so encompassing and so vital that it is amazing we in our current churches are avoiding some of its obvious implications as if the concept never existed.

All Cultures and Backgrounds

This last passage quoted above reminds us that the oneness that God seeks is not merely concerning Jew-born Christians and Gentile-born Christians, but includes all cultures and backgrounds. It is as if God dealt first with the most divergent of cultures, Jews and Gentiles, so that we are compelled now to bring together any and every kind of person in Christ with all other true believers. This is the new view that exploded on the scene following the Passion Week. It was launched into a missionary program on the day of Pentecost. In fact, the Spirit was poured out in part to accomplish this very leveling out and blending together of all cultures in Christ, as the Joel prophecy states in Acts 2.

I say "exploded" for that is exactly how it must have looked to everyone. The book of Acts is a chain reaction explosion taking place all across the known world until, as Paul affirms, the entire Roman world had heard the good news (Colossians 1:6). This intention of God to unite people of all cultures into a living unity in Christ was the ideological energy source of the new evangelism. The Jews were to be an object lesson to the world before Pentecost, not about evangelizing the world. The multi-cultural New Man, in contradistinction, is to be made up of anyone and everyone. "And it shall be that everyone [meaning anyone, not just Jews] who calls on the name of the Lord will be saved" (Acts 2:21). This is a stunning picture laid out for us, and the biggest socio-religious shift of all time. The reverberations surround us still.

This unity won by the cross was threatened by legalism, the adherence to laws about eating certain foods and feasts and circumcision and other "works of the Law" which were of external importance to Jews. As these were carried over into Christianity by some Jews and, as certain leaders promoted conformity by Gentiles, Christianity suffered and was weakened. That is the battle that had to be won in the early church, and Paul especially was committed to fighting it to its demise. It is a lion still stalking the church, as we will see.

The Church of the Future

An additional impetus to our unity among diversity is that of the projected makeup of the future kingdom. That unity is glorious when seen in the eschatological future world comprised of those from "every tribe and tongue and people and nation" (Revelation 5:11). We cannot, *must* not, live contrary to our final convergence in Christ. In the ugly slavery of early America, the schizophrenia regarding it was incredible. There were blacks and whites who would not dream of worshipping as equals, yet at the same time would hold as a doctrinal verity that all colors would be in heaven together some day. This was entirely incongruous. We are called to experience in this life as much of the spirit of unity that will characterize us in the new earth as is possible. The ideal of heaven is always to be the pursuit of earthbound believers. "Your will be done, on earth as it is in heaven" (Matthew 6:10). We cannot pray for the Kingdom to come and not relish what that coming Kingdom means. Our community of believers is to be a living demonstration of the power of the cross and also of the purified Bride who awaits the wedding. We are denying our future calling if we fail in this area. We are smearing our reputation and throwing dirt on our bridal gown.

Reminded of the race-shattering significance of the cross

over the Law and the future world, we might well read Scripture with a better perspective. It is not just a point of historical interest to converse about the early church Jew/Gentile convergence, but a matter of current necessity. This issue speaks to us now. As we look ahead to the new heaven and the new earth we are not just to long for something, but to do something about our state while on this old earth—right now.

God is glorified when we bring our diverse backgrounds together in these outposts of heaven called local churches. As one friend says, "It is God showing off." God even affirms that it is His compelling interest for the authorities in the heavenly places to see our oneness. ". . . to bring to light what is the administration of the mystery which for ages has been hidden in God who created all things; so that the manifold wisdom of God might *now* be made known *through the church* to the rulers and the authorities in the heavenly places" (Ephesians 3:9–10, NASB, emphasis mine).

What Not to Be

I will say this as strongly as I can: you should not start "a black church" or "a white church" or a "home-schooling church" or one for professional people and another for poor people. Nor should you start a church aimed at younger people or older people. In this the modern church has erred. I do not mean that we should not be evangelistic toward all these types of people, but that in building the local church our aim is too low and, frankly, sometimes selfish. We are forfeiting something of the glory of the church by not seeking to blend all kinds of people together, even if we cannot fully accomplish it. A cowboy church or a country music church may reach cowboys or country music lovers, but is this anything like what God intends to promote as the primary social implication of the cross in its victory over legalism? Does it depict real earthside yearning for a future glorious church? We have diminished the meaning of the church by doing this. Paul simply would have refused to have a Jewish church on one end of town and a Gentile church on the other.

If language barriers mean that some churches must be started for specific language groups, you must be as diverse as possible within those language groups to fulfill the intention of God. We have not fully worked out the possibilities of multi-language churches through simultaneous translating yet, but it surely would also magnify the glory of the cross and of the church if we could find some way to do so successfully.

We all know that more Hispanic people, or white people, or black people or urban poor people may be in attendance in any given church, but that is no excuse to be a "Hispanic church" or an "urban poor church." The actual demographics are God's business; ours is to seek all people in Christ, "the desire of all nations." We know that there may be more Asians in a particular part of town and that most in attendance will be from that background, but church planters must be careful not to make the church they have started to be an "Asian church." It may be Korean-speaking, if necessary, but it should not exclusively be a Korean church. If it is Christ's church, then be aware that He does not intend it to be exclusive. Do not work against the glorious cultural ramifications of the cross with your good intentions.

Even though moving from a single-culture church to a trans-cultural church (or better to a Christ-cultural church) can be a daunting task and causes many to wonder where to begin, it still must be the *intent* of the local church, and the *message* of the local church, when addressing its constituency.

I read an advertisement about a church in our city that said, "We sing the old hymns." That was all they said about themselves. What does their advertisement say concerning our objective? We all have likes and dislikes in music, but in the final analysis we really should not separate over whether old or new music is sung. This is a difficult issue and I'm not offering naive solutions. But I am saying that the gospel demands better solutions than dividing ourselves. We don't work hard enough at understanding what our separations are projecting to the world and to the heavenly authorities. As difficult as this might be, the early church had far more to work through than what music will be sung. It will be sad to face Christ in the future and say, "We could not be the glorious church You called us to be because we could not agree on the music."

One of the by-products of this kind of thinking is that some of the silliness in church life goes away. Emphasizing oneness in Christ among diverse people has a way of purifying the church. No church that is trans-cultural can make it without prayer, sound teaching, close pastoral oversight, Christ-centered worship, loving interactivity, and biblical evangelism, all of which are unifying aspects of church life. Such churches work harder at what the people have in common, the ground that is shared in Christ. When backgrounds are so divergent that there is nothing in common but Christ and the Bible, then Christ and the Bible become the subject of the conversation. Paul worked to de-emphasize cultural likes and dislikes that are inconsequential (if not downright divisive) in favor of New Covenant principles and behavior. It takes biblical thinking to get there. This was exactly what Paul was laboring at in so many of his letters.

A Bolder Proclamation

Paul asked the Ephesians to pray "that utterance may be given to me in the opening of my mouth, to make known with boldness the mystery of the gospel, for which I am an ambassador in chains; that in proclaiming it I may speak boldly, as I ought to speak" (Ephesians 6:19–20 NASB). What was he saying? He was speaking of the mystery of the shared promise, the shared inheritance for the most diverse of cultures. He did not intend to be quiet about what the cross has done. He was on a lifelong mission to bring in Gentiles, but he almost always began by teaching in synagogues, preaching the message that both Jews and Gentiles are one and must live out their oneness before the world and before the authorities in the heavenly places. We must rise above the old legalism. We must not minimalize what God has made so much of.

Trans-cultural life in the church isn't easy to come by, nor easy to maintain. It is *right,* though. And, as difficult as it would be to join followers of Christ across tribal lines when they once threatened each other with spears, who could doubt that it would redound to the glory of God if it were done. That's glory God deserves. Surely no one would deny the outrageous, hilarious glory and beauty of the urban rock music orientated believer on his face in prayer next to the traditional, white-haired, hymn-loving grandmother who has walked with God for sixty years. Heaven is glorious, and that is heaven on earth.

Biblical Sanctification
The Antidote to Legalism
"For this is the will of God, your sanctification."
(1 Thessalonians 4:3)

Rev. Richard D. Phillips

The famous first question and answer of the Westminster Shorter Catechism asks, "What is the chief end of man?" and answers, "The chief end of man is to glorify God and enjoy Him forever." It is seldom appreciated that the point of the second part of that answer—"to enjoy Him forever"—is sanctification. To better access the original intent, we might say that our chief end is "to glorify God and to enjoy pleasing Him forever," or, "to glorify God and to be enjoyed *by* Him forever." This was the Apostle Paul's point in the 4th chapter of 1 Thessalonians: "Finally, then, brothers, we ask and urge you in the Lord Jesus, that as you received from us how you ought to live and to please God, just as you are doing, that you do so more and more" (1 Thessalonians 4:1). G. K. Beale comments: "Whether in the ancient world or today, the chief end of humanity has often been to take pleasure in this life. In contrast, our passage begins by affirming the opposite: Humanity's chief goal ought to be to take pleasure in pleasing God."

As Paul states it, sanctification is not aimed primarily towards our own well-being or glory. Rather, the first goal of our sanctification, as with all things, is to give him pleasure and manifest His glory.

Sanctification Biblically Defined
Sanctification describes the process of becoming holy, *sanctus* being the Latin word for holy. *Sanctus* is joined to the Latin

187

verb *facare*, which means to make. Therefore, sanctification is the process by which believers in Christ are made holy. Paul describes it in verse 1 as a walk, by which he means an entire lifestyle: "how you ought to walk and to please God." Sanctification is a progressive work by which our lifestyle becomes more and more pleasing to God: "that you do so more and more" (1 Thessalonians 4:1).

God is holy in that He is utterly different from and higher than any other being. God's holiness especially involves His moral purity. Likewise, for us to become holy—or to be sanctified—is to be separate from sin and sinfulness, having different values than the non-believing world around us. Paul later emphasizes: "Abstain from every form of evil" (1 Thessalonians 5:22). Sanctification's attitude, therefore, is being opposed to sin and evil. This holiness is increasingly to characterize our way of living over time.

In this passage, Paul singles out the need for Christians to be morally pure with respect to the sexual perversity of the world: "For this is the will of God, your sanctification: that you abstain from sexual immorality; that each one of you know how to control his own body in holiness and honor, not in the passion of lust like the Gentiles who do not know God" (1 Thessalonians 4:3–5). Paul focuses on sexual purity not merely because this is one of God's moral expectations, but apparently because this was a sin to which the Christians in Thessalonica might be tempted. Christians are to be different especially in those areas where their own generation is most debased, which are also those areas where the world's influence will be strongest.

While sanctification involves a negative stance against sin and a separation from worldly practices, it also involves a positive exhibiting of godliness. Paul says not merely for them to abstain from sexual sin, but that "each one of you know how to control his own body in holiness and honor" (1 Thessalonians 4:4). This is true with respect to every area of life—sexuality, our treatment of others, our use of money, and our conduct in the workplace. Not only are we not to fall into worldly patterns of sin, but we are to honor God with conduct that will please and glorify Him in every aspect of life. Paul states this positive approach to sanctification in verse 7: "For God has not called us for impurity, but in holiness."

Finally, note that sanctification is bodily in expression. Holiness is rooted in our hearts, but always expressed in our actions. Notice how concrete is Paul's view of holiness and how bodily is its fulfillment. The problem with the pagans was their sensual outlook towards everything. Christians are to live "not in the passion of lust like the Gentiles who do not know God" (1 Thessalonians 4:5). In every way their lives were idolatrous, in the service of debased passions and lusts. Christians, knowing God, are to use their bodies in honorable ways in accordance with God's law, with self-control, and purity.

Sanctification: God's Sovereign Will

With this biblical introduction to sanctification—that its goal is to take pleasure in pleasing God, its method is to be separate from impurity and sin, its attitude is both negative towards sin and positive towards godliness, and its expression is concrete and bodily—we may now consider Paul's link between sanctification and the sovereignty of God. There are some who complain that a high view of God's sovereignty stands in the way of holy living. Just as people wrongly complain that the doctrine of predestination discourages evangelism, they also argue that God's sovereignty cuts off our motivation to holiness. "If God is sovereign and has chosen me to salvation," some argue, "then why should I bother living a holy life?"

1 Thessalonians 4:1–8 sets forth three responses, each of which shows that divine sovereignty in fact promotes rather than deters sanctification. The Reformed view of God's sovereignty centers everything on God's sovereign will, which Paul explains in these words: "For this is the will of God, your sanc-

tification" (1 Thessalonians 4:3). A high view of God's sovereignty promotes our zeal for holiness because we know that God has ordained our sanctification and Christians therefore know that we will be holy.

It is notable, in fact, how often the idea of holiness is found in close proximity to the Bible's statements of God's sovereign grace. Romans 8:29 says: "For those whom [God] foreknew He also predestined to be conformed to the image of His Son." The goal of predestination is not merely salvation in general terms, but specifically in terms of Christ-like holiness. Equally pointed is Ephesians 1:4: "He chose us in [Christ] before the foundation of the world, that we should be holy and blameless before Him." When the objection is made that sovereign grace inhibits a motivation for the difficult work of sanctification, Paul's answer is that we are sovereignly saved to holiness. Holiness is the mark of the elect, so that no one is warranted in thinking themselves set apart for salvation unless there is a noticeable work of sanctification taking place in their lives. Beale comments: "Those who do not break off from their former pagan ways of living should not be considered truly Christian and should certainly not be given assurance that their faith is genuine."

A humble believer asks, "How can someone like me expect to be holy?" The Bible answers, "Because it is God's sovereign will for you. You have in Christ a new identity; you are a holy one. Realizing God's calling and God's will, we are emboldened to a more active faith that is energetic in sanctification.

Sanctification: God's Sovereign Reign

There is a second way in which a high view of God's sovereignty aids in the pursuit of holiness. This has to do with sovereignty not as God's ultimate control of all things, but rather as His sovereign reign. God is sovereign over His kingdom, so that to be saved is to become His willing subject and to submit to His rule in everything.

We see this thinking in 1 Thessalonians 4:6: "That no one transgress and wrong his brother in this matter, because the Lord is an avenger in all these things, as we told you beforehand and solemnly warned you." Paul's point is that adultery is not only sinful uncleanness, but also a transgression of our brother's rights. Gene L. Green comments: "What many would view in our day as a strictly personal issue is understood by the apostle as a community issue that has eternal consequences."

We can expect the Lord (Paul means the exalted Lord Jesus as He reigns over God's kingdom) to make amends for our transgression by punishing the offender.

Paul's point is that Christians should realize that our sins will bring divine displeasures with resulting retribution. He wrote in Galatians 6:7–8: "Do not be deceived. God is not mocked, for whatever one sows, that will he also reap. For the one who sows to his own flesh will from the flesh reap corruption, but the one who sows to the Sprit will from the Spirit reap eternal life." Because the Lord sovereignly reigns over His people, we know that sin will have negative consequences, just as we will not fail to be blessed through obedience to God's will. The writer of Hebrews pointed out God's sovereign rule in his teaching on the Lord's discipline. If we grow slack in pursuing holiness, God is likely to discipline us through circumstances designed to gain our attention. Hebrews 12:10: "He disciplines us for our good, that we may share His holiness."

Moreover, if God is sovereign over His people, then we are to derive our standards and values from God's Word rather than from worldly society. Paul expresses himself in this very way, emphasizing that Christians have instructions from our sovereign Lord: "For you know what instructions we gave you through the Lord Jesus" (1 Thessalonians 4:2). Greeks would not have been troubled if the Christians followed the same loose sexual standards customary to that society. The same is increasingly true in America today. The very ideas of modesty and shame are but dim memories to many. It simply does not occur to most Americans that a couple would not enjoy sexual union shortly after their first date. To be a virgin after high school graduation is to be subjected to incredulous mockery. So why should Christians be different? Because we know that God is sovereign and that His rule establishes moral truth.

Furthermore, when we realize that Christ is sovereign, and that we are humble servants of His glorious kingdom, then the last thing we will seek is to transgress His royal laws. Obedience to God's Word will then be the watchword of our ministries and our lives. We will reason: "If Christ is going to reign through my ministry, then my ministry must be like His. It must be true and humble and godly in accordance with God's Word." "If Christ is going to honor my life, then it will be in response to my life honoring Him," we will reason (see 1 Samuel 2:30). In these ways, a high view of God's sovereignty in reigning over His holy kingdom promotes the very sanctification that, according to Paul, is God's will for us.

Sanctification: God's Sovereign Resources

Paul's teaching in this passage concludes with a statement so important that, if we fail to note it, our view of sanctification will be greatly diminished. He writes: "Therefore, whoever disregards this, disregards not man but God, who gives His Holy Spirit to you" (1 Thessalonians 4:8). First, we should notice that, as usual, Paul's view of sanctification is strongly Trinitarian: Sanctification is God the Father's will, is the rule of God the Son's kingdom, and it is empowered by God the Spirit, whom God gives through Jesus Christ. Moreover, this mention of the Holy Spirit reminds us that God's sovereignty provides us the resources we need for sanctification.

Whenever God's sovereignty is denied, or when a man-centered emphasis prevails, you will often see counterfeit holiness in the place of the genuine article. The Pharisees provided a classic example. Jesus said that they cleaned the outside of the cup, but left the inside filthy and rotten (Matthew 23:25). Something similar takes places today among legalists who replace biblical holiness with a shallow list of "do's" and "don'ts" that codify requirements not mandated by the Bible. It is true, as we have noted, that sanctification involves rejecting sin and worldliness. The problem is when holiness fails to penetrate deeply into our lives, or into what Jesus called "the weightier matters of the law" (Matthew 23:23). We do not divorce our spouses, but we do not really love them. We may tithe of our income, but like the Pharisees we derive more pride than joy from the exercise. So on it goes. Pharisees looked on others with contempt because they performed a few outward acts of piety. Modern-day legalists may cultivate very little love and completely miss the point of a life consecrated to God's glory, while feeling that they are holy because they vote correctly and avoid restaurants that serve alcohol.

How different Christianity looks when it is empowered not by human legalism, but by the indwelling power of the Holy Spirit, whose work produces supernatural levels of holiness. Paul thus prayed for the Ephesians to "know what is the hope to which he has called you, what are the riches of His glorious inheritance in the saints, and what is the immeasurable greatness of His power toward us who believe" (Ephesians 1:18–19). The power that Christians may access through faith is nothing less than "His great might that He worked in Christ when He raised Him from the dead and seated Him at His right hand in the heavenly places" (Ephesians 1:19–20). In other words, the same power that raised Jesus from dead is able to raise us up from lives of selfishness, hatred, and sin. Paul was referring to the Holy Spirit, as he made clear in Romans 8:11: "If the Spirit of Him who raised Jesus from the dead dwells in you, He who raised Christ Jesus from the dead will also give life to your mortal bodies through His Spirit who dwells in you."

A high view of God's sovereignty fuels a high aspiration for personal holiness precisely because it relies on the power God has promised in this regard. Paul says that, by the ministry of the Holy Spirit, believers are being "transformed into [Christ's] image from one degree of glory to another" (2 Corinthians 3:18). This is what gives us confidence that we can overcome our besetting sins: God will give us the Holy Spirit to overcome them. This is what makes us believe that we can display the fruit of the Spirit in ever-increasing measure: God has the power to bring it to life in our hearts. It is God's sovereign will that we should be holy; it is the rule of Christ's reign that we should obey God's Word; and it is the work of the Holy Spirit in us that empowers us to ever-higher degrees of holy living.

There is a second feature of man-centered sanctification for us to avoid: a reliance on techniques for personal growth. Evangelical bookstores abound today with five steps for this and seven steps for that. We are fasting, touching prayer cloths, and some even attempt to turn the Buddhist practice of yoga into a Christian "discipline." There are, of course, necessary Christian activities, like those of Bible-study, prayer, and the sacraments. But we must not forget that even biblically-mandated disciplines like God's word, prayer, and our worship only give power as God sovereignly causes them to do so. Therefore, we direct our hearts toward God as the One who causes the means of grace to convey the grace that we seek.

Important as Bible study and preaching are, we should never seek blessing from these activities themselves, but rather from God as we sit before His sovereign Word. As vital as prayer is, we must open our hearts to God and direct our thoughts to His throne if we expect to receive His peace. Finally, we must never think that merely having water poured over our heads or that taking the elements of the Lord's Supper into our mouths provides us with any real grace. Instead, the baptism and the Lord's Supper convey grace to us as our hearts receive Christ in faith as His saving work is sacramentally dramatized.

It is because of God's sovereign resource that Paul says that to disregard God's call to holiness is to disregard "not man but God, who gives the Holy Spirit to you" (1 Thessalonians 4:8). Since God has made such rich provision for our sanctification, what an affront it is to Him when we refuse such mighty aid, relying on earthly techniques and continuing to serve our sinful desires.

Calvinism's Record in History

As we have studied the sovereignty of God in sanctification—seeing that holiness is God's will for us, that God's sovereign rulership demands holiness, and that God's Holy Spirit sovereignly empowers a supernatural holiness—we may conclude by asking what is the record of history with respect to those who believed in the sovereignty of God in their sanctification? James Boice tackled this proposition in a chapter titled, "What Calvinism Does in History," referring to the system of doctrine noted for emphasizing God's sovereignty. In addition to considering the biblical evidence, Boice writes: "it may prove useful to consider the influence [the belief in God's sovereignty] has had on Christian history. If Calvinism is biblical, then we should expect to discover that wherever and whenever these doctrines have come under assault, the church has suffered spiritual, moral, and social decline."

At the same time, if Reformed doctrines like the sovereignty of God are biblical, we would expect spiritual power to flourish where and when these doctrines are fervently held.

As Boice shows, this is precisely the record of church history. First, he points to the record of Geneva in the time of John Calvin. It was a city known for moral debauchery, including drunkenness, gambling, prostitution, and widespread adultery. Dishonest business practices were common and blasphemy was practiced publicly. This was the situation in 1536 when young John Calvin began preaching in Geneva. At first, his ministry was unpopular and his demand for biblical obedience resulted in his dismissal. When the city had deteriorated in his absence, however, Calvin was summoned to return. He preached twice on Sunday and several times during the week, verse by verse, chapter by chapter, and book by book, teaching the Holy Scriptures. The hallmark of his teaching—following the Bible—was God's sovereignty over all things. Did "the Calvinist system of doctrine with its undying passion to see God glorified in all of life" produce moral laxity? Not at all. The effect was exactly the opposite. Boice explains:

> Daily exposure to Calvin's sound exposition of the Bible transformed the mind and heart of Geneva. The citizens embraced their election as the people of God and their calling to build a holy city. Their motto became *post tenebras lux*—"after darkness, light." As they learned to worship the God of grace... Geneva became a happier city. It also became a more wholesome city.

Another group of Christians noted for their devotion to God's sovereignty was the Puritans in seventeenth century England and Scotland. The Puritan passion was to worship God according to His Word, both in the services of the church and in all of life. They were spiritual descendants of Calvin's Geneva, having been inspired by their countrymen who fled persecution to Geneva and who returned with a commitment to the sovereignty and glory of God. The Puritans were committed Calvinists, as is seen in the Westminster Confession of Faith and Catechisms. We ask, then, if their emphasis on God's sovereignty made them lax in the matter of holiness.

The very name "Puritan" bears testimony that this was not the case. The name was meant as an insult from by those who despised their devotion to the detailed obedience of God's Word. The Puritan attitude towards life was summarized by Benjamin Wadsworth, who said, "Every Christian should do all he can to promote the glory of God, and the welfare of those about him."

The Puritans were hard workers, since they believed that Christ was sovereign not only over religious work, but over all work. They placed a high value on marriage, on the home, and on education. They were known for their charity, believing that wealth was to be used for the good of all society and not for personal pleasure. As Boice wrote: "The Puritan mind was a God-centered mind, and the result was a God-glorifying life."

The greatest American Calvinist was Jonathan Edwards, a true heir of John Calvin and a latter-day Puritan. In his book *The End for Which God Created the World,* written in 1765, he argued that God's ultimate purpose is to display His glory in all His works. It is little wonder, then, that in addition to being his generation's greatest theologian, Edwards was blessed by God with being the principle instrument by which the Great Awakening brought revival to America.

Meanwhile, our own day is one in which belief in God's sovereignty is uncommon among evangelical Christians. Would anyone seriously argue that ours is an age of great holiness? Would anyone suggest that there is a widespread passion to please God in accordance with His Word? Would anyone argue that we are benefiting from a strong wind of God's power, so that God's Word is strongly impacting society? Is it not instead the case that at this very moment when God's sovereignty is most strongly denied and neglected that the church is stained by sin, shattered by division, and so weak that, far from shaping society, the church is instead being strongly reshaped by the world? Might it be that we need a theological repentance, whereby we humble ourselves before a mighty, sovereign God?

What about Reformed Christians, those who believe and even defend the doctrines associated with God's sovereignty? Do we live with a commitment for God to be pleased through our holy lives? Have we committed ourselves to Christ's sovereign reign, as our Master and Lord? Do we rely, with expectant faith, on the sovereign power of the Spirit of holiness? By regaining not merely doctrinal assent to God's sovereignty, but an actual vision of glorifying and pleasing our sovereign God, we may learn anew His will for our lives, as Paul declared: "This is the will of God, your sanctification" (1 Thessalonians 4:3).

Other Titles from
The Northampton Press

Sermons on the Lord's Supper, by Jonathan Edwards. Contains 15 sermons by the great New England preacher, 13 of which were previously unpublished. 272 pages HB

Sermons on Important Doctrines, by John Colquhoun. A great Scottish preachers deals with justification, sanctification, salvation from sin, Christ as our righteousness, and others. 252 pages HB.

The Christian Father's Present to His Children, by John Angell James. This book shows that the best gift any father can leave his children is a godly upbringing. 326 pages HB

Heaven Taken by Storm, by Thomas Watson. Watson shows the "holy violence" required to storm the gates of heaven. 148 pages HB

Saving Faith, by John Colquhoun. This book distinguishes true faith from its counterfeits. 300 pages HB

Light and Heat: The Puritan View of the Pulpit, by Dr. R. Bruce Bickel. The best book on Puritan preaching in print today. 180 pages HB

Distinguishing Traits of Christian Character, by Gardiner Spring. What marks a man as a true child of God? Which ones cannot be counterfeited? 150 pages, HB

Studies on Saving Faith, by Arthur Pink. This is a hard-hitting rebuttal to the "easy-believism" that is so prevalent in our day. It shows that repentance is necessary for salvation. 217 pages, HB

A Dialogue Between a Catholic Priest and a Protestant, by Matthew Poole. A debate over the issues dividing these two very different faiths. 145 pages, HB.

The Precious Things of God, by Octavius Winslow. A warm devotional book that lists those things that God finds precious. 280 pages, HB.

Sighs From Hell, by John Bunyan. The author of *Pilgrim's Progress* was also a fine Bible expositor. This is his treatment of Luke 16, a story Christ told of Dives and Lazarus. It is especially timely in light of a popular mega-church pastor's book denying a literal hell. 168 pages. HB

Preparing For Eternity, by Mike Gendron. The author was a devout Roman Catholic for 34 years before God opened his eyes to biblical and doctrinal truth. He compares Romanist dogma with Scripture truth. Topics such as the proper role of Mary, the ultimate source of authority, the mass, purgatory, the sufficiency of Christ's sacrifice, and others are examined. 250 pages. PB.

Faith, by Jeremiah Burroughs. This book is comprised of two extremely scarce titles by this beloved Puritan preacher: *Precious Faith* and *The Saints' Walk by Faith,* neither of which has been in print since the 17th century. 288 pages. HB

The Natural Man's Condition, by Christopher Love. Here are sermons from Ephesians 2 on the hopelessness of being without Christ and the glorious benefits of being in Christ. Love distinguishes true hopes from false hopes. 176 pages, HB.

Let Us Pray, by MacArthur, Sproul, Piper, and others. Some of today's best Bible teachers and authors give us instruction on prayer: Why we should pray, what prayer is, what the focus of prayer is God, not ourselves, and other helpful topics. 188 pages, PB.